Waldorf Education

Christopher Clouder
Martyn Rawson

Waldorf Education

Anthroposophic Press

First published in English in 1998 by Floris Books
and Anthroposophic Press

Published by Anthroposophic Press Inc
3390 Route #9, Hudson, NY 12534

Cover photoographs by Aliki Sapountzi

ISBN 0–88010–460–0

Printed in Great Britain

Contents

Introduction

Steiner Waldorf Schools are all non-selective, multi-cultural, co-educational and offer a comprehensive curriculum. Their other unique feature is that they are all independent, self-administered community schools without internal hierarchical management structures.

This book sets out to present Steiner Waldorf educational theory and practice based on the experience of a world-wide educational movement some 75 years old and now encompassing over 700 schools, 1,500 kindergartens and some 50 teacher training institutes. The Steiner Waldorf Schools' movement is the largest group of educational institutions in the world working out of a common educational philosophy and approach.

The name *Steiner Waldorf* is a somewhat ungainly construction. The first part refers to Dr Rudolf Steiner (1861–1925), the inspiring founder of the first such school, and the second part refers to the name of that school which was known as *die Waldorfschule,* the Waldorf School. That school was founded in 1919 in Stuttgart in southern Germany to provide education for the children of the workforce at the Waldorf-Astoria cigarette factory. The curriculum developed for that first school, and the subsequent movement that has grown out of that original initiative has retained the name *Waldorf.* Many such schools around the world use the name *Waldorf* in their title, such as the Bristol Waldorf School in England; the Harduf Waldorf School in Nazareth-Elit, Israel; Inkanyezi Waldorfcentre in Johannesburg; the Colegio Waldorf in Lima, Peru; or the Chicago Waldorf School. Many other schools call themselves Rudolf Steiner Schools, or just Steiner Schools. In reality all these schools share essentially the same philosophy and basic curriculum, so the term *Steiner Waldorf* has increasingly been used as a kind of collective term.

Kindergarten building at the Raphael House Waldorf School, Wellington, New Zealand

Steiner Waldorf Schools are evolving social organisms that stand in a reciprocal relationship to their cultural environment. They have to adapt to increasingly diverse circumstances and make a significant contribution to their evolving social context. That they have survived at all is a testimony to the courage and devotion of many individuals. What is presented here is a depiction of how they appear at the present and a tentative prognosis of their future. For all of them the child is central.

To begin to show what Waldorf education has become in our times we would like to start by taking a glimpse into the life of a typical Steiner Waldorf School in our home country of Britain. What follows is a picture in words of Waldorf education at work.

1. A school festival

Chinks of light escape through the improvised blackout. The room is full and expectant. Packed tightly together on school chairs sit mothers, fathers, grandparents, brothers and sisters. Around the back, adults stand with toddlers in arms. At the front on benches and cross-legged on the floor huddle children clutching wooden swords and wearing horned helmets of finest cardboard and silver paint. The stage curtain bulges, whispers can be heard. A teacher and the spotlight seek each other momentarily. The crowded room quickly becomes quiet without anyone calling for silence. The festival is about to begin.

For the next hour or more, class after class of children from the youngest to the oldest take to the stage and present something they have been working on to the school community. There is music of all kinds and at many levels amid a bewildering and seemingly effortless interchange of music stands, instruments, sheet music, players and conductors. With deep empathy we give our support to a class of first graders performing on recorders for the first time, their wide eyes glued on the teacher's fingers. We marvel at the somewhat older recorder consort. The range of recorders matched only by the extreme range of the players' heights. All those tall girls and little boys, they must be sixth graders, too busy to have really noticed the onset of puberty, yet! And later we are charmed by the youthful trio playing Mozart with the kind of verve professionals try very hard to achieve, their casual self-consciousness unhindered by their equally relaxed dress sense. Why do concert performers wear bow-ties and off the shoulder velvet dresses from some ancient fashion epoch? These young musicians

Celebrating the Olympic Games in Class 5

evoke the spirit of Mozart more than adequately in Doc Martens and black T-shirts.

There is drama, too, in various languages. A horde of fourth grade berserkers rise from the darkness of the hall to stamp onto the stage and impress us with their remarkable command of alliteration. Thor, though one of the smallest in the class, has an enormous voice to match the famous Thor's Hammer, passed on down the generations of fourth graders. The bit where Thor dresses as a girl and then knocks the taunting warriors off their benches in well choreographed waves of destruction, is particularly impressive. The warriors, their cardboard horns somewhat crestfallen, are in good heart, however, and greet the thunderous applause with jaunty gestures to their friends until they are shepherded off-stage by a couple of no-nonsense stagehands from the ninth grade.

This feature length performance leaves only time for a

complex but brief story of everyday farming life in French, involving various farm creatures crowing and squeaking with excellent accents and a very bossy farm wife, with hands on hips, ordering her husband around in convincing colloquial terms. They say children learn through imitation, but who could she possibly be imitating?

Other languages we hear, though we in the audience do not all understand, included passages of the book of Genesis recited in Hebrew, the alphabet and some lines from Homer's *Odyssey* in Ancient Greek and three short, intense word pictures in Paul Cellan's German, spoken by a group of high school students, some of whom reappear minutes later in silk costumes to perform eurythmy to a dramatic piece of piano music by Rachmaninov full of Russian passion and deep swelling emotion. The boys who perform the bass parts make up in striding dignity what they lack in grace as they enter and leave the stage.

Thor and his hammer   *Playing the recorder*

The programme is completed by a powerful recitation of Martin Luther King's *I have a dream* speech by a chorus of ninth graders, followed by the whole school orchestra efficiently assembling in next to no time to perform one movement of the Haydn symphony they are preparing for the annual concert later in the year.

As the parents file out of the hall and the pupils scamper back to their classrooms to disrobe or put their instruments away, a cheerful sound of conversation can be heard. In the school entrance stand exhibition panels showing charcoal drawings, mostly abstract but with a few gaunt trees against cold skies, a city skyline in silhouette and a strange view down what looks like dungeon steps with finely shaded shadows. There are water colour landscape paintings, some with skies that would not be out of place in an exhibition of German Expressionists.

On tables are arranged a row of stone carvings, showing careful curves and sensitive hollows. Before them stands a circle of copper bowls, from tall and thin to full and round. On the next table two wooden boxes with beautiful dovetail joints at the corners sit on brightly coloured woven rugs. Beside that table stands another with a solid looking tool box with a dozen or so tools fanned out in front. On second glance it becomes apparent that these tools mostly have newly turned wooden handles, but that the metal parts were old iron with brightly ground and polished cutting or sawing edges. A note explains that this set of tools has been repaired and restored and are about to be shipped off, as a carpenter's tool-kit to Mozambique.

A celebration and a re-creation

This festival and the exhibition of work was presented by a Steiner Waldorf School, one of its regular termly school festivals at which the children and teachers show the parents what they have been working on in their lessons. These are not performances as such, the school calendar has quite enough of those with plays, concerts, eurythmy perfor-

A Lower School orchestra

mances throughout the year. Many of the activities shown
on stage are adaptations of what goes on in the classroom,
indeed sometimes enterprising teachers will reconstruct a
classroom situation on stage. Such festivals are a celebration
of the work. Essentially aimed at the parents and friends,
the festivals also provide a valuable educational experience
for the pupils. Not only is there a certain raising of consciousness for the activities, there is a certain pride in presenting what one can do. Above all, however, the younger
children can look up with awe and expectation at what the
older pupils can do, and the older ones can look back with
fond and sometimes embarrassed memories on their own
earlier childhood. Not only do such festivals engender a
warm community spirit, but they offer a biographical sense
of continuity to the children (and perhaps the adults too).
There is nothing competitive, there are no prizes. There is

only a celebration of school work in which individual and group, each according to their abilities, can participate and be appreciated.

The festival we have described above may be typical of festivals in many other Steiner Waldorf Schools around the world. The venues may differ, from wonderfully designed school theatres to a semi-derelict warehouse, reflecting the incredible diversity of circumstances in which we find such schools. The languages and cultural context will vary too, since there are Steiner Waldorf Schools in over forty differ ent countries around the world. Some old established schools will put on breathtakingly professional perform- ances, other newer, smaller schools will be much more modest. But visitors are always surprised at the standard of the presentations, at the imaginative ways in which things are done, and they are moved by the commitment and motivation of the children.

Of course, many schools other than Steiner Waldorf Schools are proud of their performances. What differences are there? What is distinctive about a festival at a Steiner Waldorf School? What does such a festival tell us about this kind of school?

Well, firstly, the items presented are inspired by an age-specific curriculum. Almost any age of child could in theory perform a play based on Norse mythology. In a Steiner Waldorf School this would belong to a class of ten year olds because within the overall context of the curriculum the Norse myths represent themes and evoke a mood speci- fically relevant to this age group. Likewise, Martin Luther king's speech expresses the impassioned idealism of fifteen years olds in a way that the story of Thor's hammer would not. Ten year olds, on the other hand, lack the emerging sense of burning injustice and asserted identity that King's words express. The point we wish to make here is that the teachers have chosen material and presented it in such a way that the differing age groups can engage in a particular and appropriate manner. Naturally there is more to Norse myth or Martin Luther King than ten or fifteen years olds could ever grasp. The very depth inherent in such cultural

Mary and the donkey in a Mexican Nativity play

material stimulates the children in a profound way that often works on beyond the immediate experience.

The second aspect that needs to be taken into account is the method of teaching which is exemplified by the styles of presentation by each age group in the festival. This method is also age specific. The nine year olds acting out the French play, singing songs and reciting text in chorus, all of which they have learned by ear, is typical of the way foreign languages are taught to children in the age range of seven to nine. The other items on the programme equally demonstrate much about the teaching techniques used with the different age groups. We will be describing such methods and the reasons behind them in the course of the book.

A third and perhaps less visible aspect is the fact that each festival is embedded in a cycle of festivals which mark not only the outer changing seasons of the year but express the inner mood of the spiritual calendar. Naturally, spring songs and poems are sung or recited which celebrate that

season but the more inwardly experienced awareness of
death and renewal, of the Passion and the Resurrection in
Christian terms, is expressed in an artistic way. The older
the children are, the more conscious and reflective the
reference to this spiritual experience. The public festival has
its reflection in the work done by each class teacher with
their own class to bring about a mood of challenge and the
need for wakefulness at Michaelmas, of the inner light
being kindled through Advent and so on through the year.
The work of the teachers together as a group searching each
year to deepen the collective understanding of the true
meaning of the cycle of the year is supported and strengthened by the meditative work of each individual on their
own spiritual path.

    Such festivals are not merely placed on convenient dates
in the school diary but are part of a cyclical and evolving
process. Festivals are both celebration and re-creation. Like
religious rituals, such festivals reinforce shared values,
strengthen the sense of community and mark development
through time. But such festivals are also linked to the
intuitive realm of the future through the creative artistic
medium. In an age in which traditional forms of ritual and
community are fading, the Steiner Waldorf Schools strive
to cultivate a new, free consciousness of time, human
development and community.

    Of course there is much more to a Steiner Waldorf
School than its festival. Many more things go on in a
school than can be presented in a termly festival, such as
the intricacies of projective geometry, the complexities of
philosophy, or the technicalities of a scientific experiment.
Nor can one show a therapeutic session, a teachers' meeting
or a class discussion, all of which are equally typical of
daily life in a Steiner Waldorf School.

    What all Steiner Waldorf Schools have in common is an
educational approach which is radically child-centred and is
based on the on-going study of the developing human being.
We shall discuss below what this means in detail.

2. Child development

What is education for?

This may seem an odd question but it is one that produces surprisingly little consensus. Essentially, though, most would agree that education has two primary functions: enabling children to cope with life in the adult world and providing society with young people with the necessary skills to meet society's needs. There may be other require- ments, such as giving children a moral training for their own salvation and for the good of society, or preserving standards of culture. The first two, however, remain central to most people's idea of what education is for. Whatever concern there is and has been for moral values for their own sake, the predominant point of view has been utilitar- ian, however ideologically this has been promoted. Educa- tion is a practical necessity for modern society. This view has been somewhat more in evidence than the equally con- temporary idea of education as a basic human right.

It would be fair to say that most philosophers of educa- tion as well as most of its practitioners have tended towards the idealistic rather than utilitarian view. Nevertheless, it tends to be politicians and bureaucrats who control the purse strings and their view of the needs of the individual and society tend to consider the needs of the state as para- mount. The concept of a free education, not merely in the sense of being freely available and accessible, but more im- portantly free in the sense that it serves no higher objectives than the free development of the individual, has not taken root everywhere. Indeed there are only a few nations who fully subscribe to the view that education should be wholly free in that sense, though there are many who go a long way further than the British Government.

Steiner Waldorf Schools strive to realize the ideal of a free education in that they place the development of the individual at the centre of their pedagogy. But in doing so they do not neglect the needs of society. In order to understand how these schools seek to find the appropriate balance between the individual and the community, we need to examine what issues face any form of education in our times.

The importance of childhood

Childhood is the most important time of our lives. In a person's life there is no more decisive phase for the development of the whole human being. The outcome of this development is not predetermined, hence the impor-

developmental stages,
recapitulation of human evolution

tance of upbringing and education. The extent to which we, as adults, can shape the course of our lives through conscious effort is bound up with the faculties we have acquired in childhood. Of course we can continue to learn and develop new skills beyond childhood but the ability to do so and the creative energy required are both strongly influenced by how we have lived our early years. In many ways children recapitulate in their development the key stages in human evolution. They do so not in a literal way but qualitatively in terms of their developmental stages. In childhood we acquire the characteristics which in evolutionary terms made us human in the first place. What humanity achieved over several million years, each child manages within the first few years: uprightness and the free use of the hands, language and cognition. Building on these fundamental human faculties, we equip ourselves for life and in so doing we further deepen our humanity. Seeds of experience are sown which germinate, grow and come to fruition later in life. In childhood what we experience forms the basis for our adult attitudes to the world and other people, for better or worse.

Childhood is of necessity a self-centred time of life. Children must first feel at home in their own growing bodies. Then they must master the co-ordination of their limbs and the organs of speech so that they can become responsive instruments of the emerging personality. In order to feel secure they must feel themselves to be the focal point of adult and family attention and from there orientate themselves within the wider world. Only a person who has found their own individual identity can stand firmly on their own two feet and not be disorientated and knocked off balance by life's storms. A person who has gained this inner sense of knowing who they are can then transform this natural and healthy self-centredness into a true altruism later in life in the service of others without the loss of their identity.

Learning to cope with one's destiny is crucial. Developing a strong self-confidence through coming to terms with the gifts and disabilities we are born with is a central task

Smoothing out the rough edges

of growing up. If we can establish a healthy relationship to ourselves when we are still young, coping with adult life will be that much easier. An honest look at ourselves and a compassionate look at those around us will reveal that many adults are still trying to overcome their sense of inadequacy and insecurity. There are many of us who have not outgrown our puberty! Indeed there are many aspects of our society that pander to an unresolved adolescence with comical and self-indulgent consequences. If not transformed by maturity, the drives of sex and power which naturally arise in puberty can lead to tragedy and mayhem. This point can scarcely be over-stated. The task then of upbringing and education is to provide a supportive environment in which the developing individual can find their way into the world with confidence and a healthy sense of themselves.

Finding meaning in the world

The natural sense of wonder and curiosity of childhood, if allowed to grow, transforms into the lifelong interest and enthusiasm that forms the heart of any quest for knowledge. It is this that always makes life interesting and counteracts boredom and frustration. If this childhood curiosity is stifled or channelled into meaningless pursuits, it can lead to a profound sense of disappointment, disillusionment and inner withdrawal. We do not have to look far today to find symptoms of inward 'emigration,' that is to say, withdrawal from life's challenges, especially amongst young people. It is not uncommon to find youngsters for whom life holds no interest, who have become cynical or apathetic, and others who seek meaningful experiences in self destructiveness such as in the obsessive world of youth cults or drugs. And it is not only teenagers who suffer through a loss of interest in life. How many adults in the middle of their lives experience a crisis of purpose and lose interest in the things they have previously held to be so important? How many people on reaching retirement don't know what to do with themselves?

A genuine connection to the world, once made in childhood, remains a resource to call upon throughout life. Through the guidance of parents and educators, children can find genuine interest in the world around them and in human culture but only if their curiosity is met with real meaning. It is a natural part of self-development to have doubt, to have questions. The difference between doubt and cynicism is that one can always seek answers to the important questions. In seeking lies hope and hope motivates the quest. The cynic no longer believes that there are answers or knows that life intrinsically has meaning.

It is the task of educators to show children the path to a meaningful understanding of the world — and not merely to hollow oversimplifications or concepts that are remote and abstract. Knowledge must nourish and to do so it must be inexhaustible. It must be based on a living relationship to the world and it must always be in context. Abstractions are complete in themselves, they cannot grow and transform as living ideas.

Facing the bad, finding the good

Not everything a child encounters in life will be good. As accurately portrayed in the images of fairy tales, mythology and traditional legend, there is much darkness and evil in the world. But facing the bad and sad things in life need not lead to pessimism. An optimistic outlook is founded on facing up to the bad, the inharmonious and the evil and yet also being able to recognize the good, the positive and the fruitful ways of life. Often we can't answer the question 'Is it right?' We can, however, ask 'Is it fruitful?'

Children assume that what adults devote themselves to

Engaging the imagination in lessons

is good and true. Such is their trust that young children will willingly imitate a sense of reverence for the things the adults around them deem important or special. This feeling goes very deep in young children — it is as though they were thirsty for such experiences. It is in the nature of early childhood to be absorbed, one might say devoted, to the activities they are engaged in. One expects adults who are role models for children to revere appropriate and meaningful aspects of life.

This devotion and reverence forms an indelible background colouring to all subsequent experience, transforming itself into a profound respect for the important things in life. It is the basis of a religious mood that permeates the significant events in an individual's biography but which enables a person to express their religious experience in any way they choose. It can provide a sound basis for an awareness of the numinous or spiritual dimensions to life experiences. If children, however, are set no worthy examples or if they experience no sense of reverence or even respect in the people they look up to, they will need to be of exceptionally strong character to acquire these feelings as adults.

With traditional social values, organized religions and creeds in decline or dominated by fundamentalism, it is, as the American poet-musician Bob Dylan put it so succinctly, 'Easy to see without looking too far that not much is really sacred!' Parents and educators have a weighty responsibility to see that the children in their care learn the right kind of respect and learn to distinguish between those things worthy of devotion and those which are superficial and transient.

In an increasingly uncertain world, where families are often split, where traditional social structures appear to be unravelling, an inner certainty of purpose can be a great help. It is a central task of education to give children not only a sense of identity but a profound sense of purpose. Is it hopelessly idealistic to think that the rising generation could face the world and its problems with some sense of service? Shouldn't a young person leaving school and going into life have the question: what does the world need and what do I need to do to develop the skill to help?

Reverence for nature on a farm visit

A developmental approach

Steiner Waldorf education believes in taking the whole human being into account and practises a developmental approach to the teaching. This educational approach takes its starting point from the careful observation of the nature of the growing and evolving human being seen in his or her physiological, psychological and spiritual aspects. It views education as a concern of life itself and draws its lessons from the inner nature of the child rather than any merely theoretical or ideological considerations. The growing up and maturing of a human being is a deeply complex matter.

Experience has shown that at different ages children benefit from a succession of learning modes. These relate specifically to the 'how' of teaching as much as to the 'what.' The differing modes take account of the psychological and cognitive stages of development the children have reached and are designed to create a flexible and supportive environment. In most situations the teaching method has primacy over the content of the lessons, though of course both form a whole. The unfolding of the subject material must match the child's level of consciousness as well as their technical ability. We will give some examples below which show how the teaching modes vary in the different age groups, though no description can do justice to the complex human interactions that make up learning situations.

Steiner Waldorf education takes both factors, the child's developmental needs and the cultivation of faculty through subject content and school experience, and integrates them in its curriculum. Children are taught in age groups with their peers in undifferentiated classes. That means there is always a wide range of ability in any class. This has considerable significance for the social development of the children. Being in mixed ability groups has the obvious — though by no means easy to achieve — social value of learning to appreciate the other person's gifts and to support them in their weaknesses, especially where the competitive element is not in the foreground. Competition can be a healthy motivation when it is self directed — namely, when the individual thinks 'Can I do better than I did last time?' Rather than 'Can I do better than them?'

The pupils in a Steiner Waldorf class often have a relationship akin to members of a family. Like families, these relationships are not always easy. Children learn from and through and occasionally in spite of each other. Learning to deal with each others' inherited gifts and weaknesses, social circumstances and emerging personalities is an education in itself, the best possible preparation for the trials and tribulations of adult personal relationships. Left to their own devices, of course, a *Lord of the Flies* situation can develop where there is an absence of sufficient inner and outer moral authority. It is not inevitable that it will work

out. This is where the class teacher and supporting staff
are vital. The teacher is role model, authority, facilitator,
referee, confessor and, when the children are young, their
conscience. In short the teacher represents social, moral and
ethical values. It is curious how many societies lack respect
for the teaching profession whilst expecting education to
generate the moral values society expects.

The curriculum has a horizontal and a vertical structure
to it. All the subjects taught in one year are integrated within larger themes which stand as motifs for that age. The
tenor of each year's curriculum is guided by the developmental needs of the children at that age. Each subject is in
this sense a part of a whole.

As the children grow and move up the school from year
to year, from class to class, they naturally encounter the
same subjects or rather the development of each subject.
This forms a kind of spiral learning experience. Each time
the child returns to a subject, there is the opportunity for the
child's experience to broaden and deepen as well as building on previous memories that both the children and their
teacher have shared

This is why many subjects are taught in periods of three
to four week blocks, then dropped for a while and picked
up again later. This rhythm of immersion in a theme, say
local geography or Roman history, then allowing it to settle,
to sink down into the background, is a key feature of
Steiner Waldorf education. The interludes between periods
are seen as phases of unconscious activity within the learning process during which the individual forms a different,
more habitual relationship to skills and faculties acquired.
Just as experiences from the day are 'processed' by the
mind during sleep, returning altered, more coherent, in some
way deepened and enhanced, when we come to ourselves in
the morning, so too the longer rhythms of the main lesson
blocks. The more engaged the child in the learning process
whilst awake, the more profound the working of the night,
the maturing process in the unconscious. Any model that
sees learning as simply input and output of information fails
to take account of the real nature of the human being,

ignores the transformative quality of experience and deni-
grates the art of education. Working actively with the process of remembering and forgetting is a unique feature of
Steiner Waldorf education.

An inner link is maintained from the naive experiences
in the kindergarten to the scientific and logical discoveries
of the Upper School. Not only does the subject grow
together with the individual but there is a metamorphosis of
childhood experience into adult knowledge. The more profound and true to the being of the phenomenon the young
child's experience is, the more profound the conscious
knowledge in later years. Wonder felt in childhood towards
nature can become the deepest sense of thoughtful responsibility in adulthood.

That is what it means when Steiner Waldorf education
says it is child-centred and follows a developmental curriculum. It doesn't mean that the child chooses what it learns.
The teacher, like a good gardener, must provide the best
possible conditions and nourishment for the child. The curriculum and all the real-life experiences that go with it
provide the substance for the child's psychological and
spiritual development. The teacher provides an environment
which is structured in the right way for the age and through
the teaching method a supportive means to learning.

A long childhood

The most obvious and also one of the most significant as
pects of growing up is that it takes such a long time. Indeed
some may feel that the process never really ends. In
general, however, we can take the traditional 'coming of
age' at twenty-one as a sign that the first great phase of life,
childhood and adolescence, is over. In nature most animals
attain maturity relatively quickly and are from that point on
fixed in their behaviour. Furthermore the attainment of
sexual maturity usually signals the end of growth and development. From that point on, most animals have to all intents
and purposes arrived at their finished state. Fortunately,

that is far from being the case with people who not only go on growing after sexual maturity but undergo further significant psychological development. Interestingly, those animals that have a relatively extended childhood, such as the higher mammals like elephants, dolphins and the great apes, do retain some capacity to go on learning into adulthood.

The young of such higher mammals — and this is true of many other animals too — are so endearing to us precisely because they exhibit for a short time such human-like behaviour and in particular that quintessential quality of childhood — playfulness. In people this playfulness continues into adulthood to a high degree. True laughter and the enigmatic smile are uniquely human traits. Mature animals, even though they can clearly enjoy themselves, rarely exhibit anything resembling play in its true sense.

Transformed into the various forms of creativity, play raises mankind beyond necessity. It is not out of any biologically determined necessity that a sonata is composed, nor does it help in the struggle for survival to write a poem about mist in the trees, neither does it help to perpetuate our genes to cultivate roses — all of which people can do without any expectation of reward or advantage. The point here is that after maturity animals apparently do little or nothing that is not biologically predetermined. The pressures of survival and selection of the fittest leave little room for creativity of the kind we associate with people. Play and creativity show us the extent to which human beings have emancipated themselves from such genetically programmed behaviour.

Self-determination?

The modern school of thought called sociobiology, or Darwinian psychology, would totally disagree. To the scientists who promote this view, there is only biological determination. All human behaviour, however altruistic, spontaneous, artistic or just plain crazy, is prompted by preconditioned

Jean-Jacques Rousseau   *John Locke*

responses designed to further the perpetuation chances of
our genes. This form of reductionism which basically sees
all human faculty as innate or inborn, requiring only the appropriate stimulus to emerge, is a remarkably influential
theory. Its thinking lies behind the ambitions of the Human
Genome Project which its supporters claim will reveal 'half
of the total knowledge of the human organism ... in five to
seven years, and all of it by the end of the decade.'[1]

This Nativist view has a long pedigree, going back to
Jean-Jacques Rousseau, but so does its opposite, the
Environmentalist view, which goes back to John Locke. The
modern version, known as behaviourism, sees the development of the child as being almost entirely determined or
programmed by environmental factors, foremost being
parents and teachers.

Steiner Waldorf education takes a different view. It sees
the development of the human being as a far more complex

and integrated phenomenon than the reductionist views of modern Darwinists or Behaviourists. Of course the genetic inheritance is a powerful force in influencing, through pre-determining certain propensities, the life of any individual, but it is not the only factor at work. Apart from the significant role played by the environment, there is another factor for which modern anthropology has yet to agree a consistent term. Even the most literally-minded sociobiologist could not deny that two sisters with practically identical genetic material, brought up in the same family, eating the same food and so on, can and often do turn out to be very different people. Of course one can always find differences in the upbringing, such as the father favouring one daughter over the other, to account for the differences, the personalities, but common sense and observation tell us that the sisters are different because they are simply different people! They are different in spite of a common inheritance and in spite of all the variable nuances of environmental influence. The processes of maturation, of growing up and of individuation are by their very nature individual.

The individuality factor

The whole period of maturation, which lasts some twenty years and more, is characterized by an inner core of individuality coming ever more clearly to expression through bodily processes and stages of psychological development common to all. The third factor in growing up, beyond heredity and environment, is the individuality of the child itself. The struggles and crises each individual goes through, and the otherwise inexplicable talents that reveal themselves, are expressions of that individuality bringing itself to ever clearer expression. Though such struggles such as childhood illnesses or the agonies of puberty may be typical for the age, the intensity with which they are suffered and probably their timing are related to the emerging personality. Only so much is genetically determined in humans, only so much experience is the direct result of environmental,

cultural or socio-economic factors. In the end there is always something more. There is always something individual about the emergence of personality, the expression of ability, the rate of learning or even the inclinations, likes and dislikes. There is even something basically inexplicable about an individual's bodily features, especially the face and eyes, which are always more than the combination of inherited features — features that become more individual with age.

The development of the individual is not merely the unfolding of something that, at least in all its essentials, is already there. Nor is it a kind of jigsaw puzzle that just needs reconstructing by some prescient force. Development is often understood by modern anthropology as synonymous with change. We have rightly freed ourselves from the earlier view of evolution as being identical with the upward march of progress which was the dominant assumption at the beginning of the twentieth century but which has become increasingly unfeasible in the light of the history of that century. But to see human development, in particular, as mere change is to miss something essential about people.

Human development, as understood by the approach taken by Steiner Waldorf education, is rather seen as a dynamic process. This begins, of course, with a basis that is given or inherited. An inner principle of being works through this basis to transform it into a higher level of completeness and in so doing brings itself more strongly and clearly to expression. This naturally occurs within a given human social and cultural context in interaction with other people who themselves are at some stage of dynamic development. Every human being experiences within themselves the urge to become more than they already are. The urge towards self-development is a central feature of our being human. The human being is only really fully human when they are striving to bring their essential and individualized humanity to higher expression. To quote Bob Dylan once more, 'He not busy being born, is busy dying.' The formulation is somewhat drastic but the idea expresses something fundamental about our being human. We are either taking hold of what life has given us and are striving to raise it to a higher, more human level, or we are regressing, falling back into the blind determinism of socio-biology's cold-blooded world of biological necessity.

It depends on how we understand life and its meaning. Education has a different perspective if we see the world as Richard Dawkins recently described it:

> In a universe of electrons and selfish genes, blind physical forces and genetic replication, some people are going to get hurt, other people are going to get lucky, and you won't find any rhyme or reason in it, nor any justice. The universe we observe has precisely the properties we should expect if there is at bottom no design, no purpose, no evil and no good, nothing but pitiless indifference.[2]

If, however, we see some purpose, namely the task to enhance consciousness and thereby change the universe, then we shall educate with a different inner intention.

3. Early years education

Play is the serious work of childhood

Play is the quintessential activity of children. It is the serious work of childhood. In play children learn to experience the possibilities and parameters of life. However natural play may be, after a while it too needs guidance and adult input. Play needs nourishing with fertile ideas that the children can then endlessly elaborate on. Without such helpful guidance play can become chaotic or even destructive since it is driven by powerful forces that we as adults can hardly comprehend. Creative play awakens and harnesses the power of imagination.

For a young child the imagined world can have more reality than the actual world — a simple piece of wood can become a flying horse, a fire-engine or a mother calling her children in for supper. This is because the human being experiences the world in the form of narrative. The young child is naturally the central figure in the story and play recreates and orders the world in the familiar forms that narratives take, with beginnings, sequences of events (e.g. then that happened, then that ...) and endings or consequences. Modern research has confirmed what the Russian psychologist Vygotsky theorized, that language development is the precondition for cognitive development and that both are based on narrative structure.

We order the world by telling stories — to ourselves and to others. Our consciousness is a stream of narrative with which we identify ourselves. A story told from the heart, however simple its content, always has more meaning to a young child than the most wonderful tale told by a disem-

Story time in kindergarten

bodied voice heard through earphones — for the simple reason that a living person is engaged in telling it. What the child 'hears' is more than the content of the story, the child also perceives the individuality of the story-teller at work.

The mental skills we learn through storytelling and play become the basis for creative thinking, problem-solving and above all the ability to grasp complex concepts. Play by its very nature involves a process of experimentation and discovery. Play starts from a given situation but the outcome is unknown. There is always more potential than can ever be realized. That is what stimulates the imagination and engages the individuality. The raising of play to the level of the highest forms of creativity in adult life is a transformation that has not always been recognized in its full significance. More and more educational psychologists are becoming aware of the many subtle stages this transformation goes

Kindergarten scenes

through, though unfortunately too few of these insights inform educational practice.

Many children today are confronted by toys where little or nothing is left to stimulate the imagination, one need only press the button to start it. There is little wonder that the child is soon bored, becomes destructive and sooner rather than later demands attention.

Play is something that engages the whole human being, especially in the young child where each thought and emotion has its accompanying movements and gestures. How passive therefore is television watching since even the eye muscles can no longer keep pace with the rapidity of the electronic images. Real play is hard work and after a intensive day's playing, children are healthily tired and ready for bed. Unfortunately many children suffer from hyperactivity, lack of concentration and are poor sleepers — problems not only for the children themselves but for stressed parents too. Could it be that there is a link between the lack of healthy play, rhythm, moral example and restless behaviour in the child? It is a modern tragedy that many children can no longer play and must be carefully taught by trained professionals. Play therapy is increasingly called for.

Lost childhood re-found

Neil Postman rang timely alarm bells back in the early eighties with his book *The Disappearance of Childhood* in which he portrayed the modern American child as a television watching consumer, as a miniature though not yet opinioned citizen, without appropriate time or space to develop in. This vision of the child shocked many. Indeed our society, though outwardly professing to consider childhood a vital time of life, conspires to rob children of their birthright — the right to be a child.

We are often ambiguous towards children. By treating them as little adults capable of judgments — 'Do you want to go to bed now?' 'Do you want to live with Mummy or Daddy?' — we only make them feel unheld, formless, vulnerable. By exposing them to unsuitable media we deprive them of the initiative to explore the world in play, and flood their still unprotected senses so that the clear perception on which sound judgment is based is lacking. By offering no clear guidance, or exposing them to our own inadequacies and doubt, we deprive them of a secure emotional environment. By forcing them to grow up too quickly, paradoxically we prevent true maturity from developing. An individual who loses trust in the world too soon, who has not learned to love learning, cannot easily love work. Above all, depriving children of the time it takes to learn to love and respect others, makes it so much harder for the individual to form healthy relationships. By subjecting children to our own neuroses we perpetuate a vicious circle. As the journalist Susie Orbach of the *Guardian* put it:

> What we so often fear in children is their needs. If we get it wrong, children may be overwhelmed by feelings of vulnerability and neediness. They easily sense when adults cannot handle such things straightforwardly ... To be sure, children need guidance and structures. But these need to be structures of caring, structures which are stable and which are responsive to what children do and what children are. Our sentimentality towards children is often a counterpoint to our fear that we can't provide what it is that our children need from us.[3]

The ethos of a Steiner Waldorf kindergarten is to be responsive to what children are and provide them with the next best thing after a loving family, an environment where children can develop their childhood. The age between birth and the second dentition, around the age of six to seven, is the most formative period of any individual's life. From the age of three onwards children can begin to socially interact with children of their own age and benefit from the opportunities provided by a playgroup and then kindergarten.

With the basics of language more or less established children between the ages of three and five develop two new faculties that change their relationship to their surroundings — memory and imagination. This enables children to re-create, particularly in play, things and situations they have experienced. Kindergarten gives the children ample opportunity to engage in the constructive play by providing lots of natural objects, rather than finished toys, which the children can transform into whatever their memories and imaginations require. The mental activity is important. As Steiner put it:

> As the muscles of the hand grow firm and strong in performing work for which they are fitted, so the brain and other organs of the physical body are

guided along the right lines of development if they
receive the right impressions from the environment.[4]

Life in a day in kindergarten

A Steiner Waldorf Kindergarten is like an extended family.
The day and its activities have a regular rhythm and
structure from the children's arrival until their departure.
There is a balance between the daily work that needs to be
done, caring for the house, baking the bread, doing the
washing and so on as well as handicrafts such as simple
weaving, carving, embroidery and sewing. There is sweep-
ing to be done, leaves gathered up outside and even a little
garden to tend. Then of course there are the festivals to
celebrate, stories to be told, songs to be sung and games to
be played. Last and by no means least, there is time for
creative play both indoors and outdoors.

A Whitsun festival in the kindergarten

Visitors may be surprised to see just how busy the children are in a kindergarten, surprised also perhaps to see the children working with hammers and saws, kneading heavy dough or rolling large logs up and down in the garden. 'Make-believe' may be an important part of play but it seems real enough. Nor are the children merely left to play. The role of the kindergarten leader may be unobtrusive but it is one that requires long training and preparation to be effective in leading by example.

The kindergarten staff spend hours in their kindergartens both before the children arrive in the morning and after they have gone. There are activities and materials to prepare, of course, but more importantly there has to be the right mood in the place. The staff often meet in the morning to say a verse together before making their presence felt in the rooms before the first children appear.

Painting in the kindergarten

As the children begin to arrive, the kindergarten leader is already busy so that the children, having hung up their coats and changed their shoes, can be given a homely welcome. At first there may be a period of free play with small groups of children choosing their area, either getting the dolls up and dressed, building with wooden blocks or driving a bus made from an upturned chair. The adults are usually engaged in some task, perhaps preparing the dough if it is a baking day. There is conversation and some of the children may prefer to be around the adults, as children traditionally have been, watching, 'helping' while adults work, asking questions and so on. These informal moments are vital, not least in a world in which every one is often so busy.

The adults initiate the next phase by beginning to clear the things away and the children join in helping each tool or object to find its place on shelf or in basket. The forces of imitation are strongest at this age and can be most easily directed when the adults perform their tasks in a conscious and careful way, repeating the gestures of each action in a rhythmical and natural way. Children can learn to do quite complex practical tasks, even involving sharp or awkward tools or equipment, if they see them regularly performed with love and care.

Tidying up is an important task and it is done in such a way that it does not occur to the children that this is something which spoils their fun or is a tedious chore. Once things have been put back in their places, the children gather for ringtime during which traditional songs are sung, rhythmical verses are spoken and acted out. Sometimes the eurythmist or foreign language teacher may visit and contribute to the circle's activities. These activities help focus the children's attention and especially strengthen their linguistic skills. Listening and clear articulation can be exercised through this kind of rhythmical recitation. Afterwards, the children go to the toilet and wash their hands. Some of the older ones who are first back help lay and set the table with place-mats, cutlery and perhaps a vase of flowers. Bread is cut and everyone gathers to say a grace and sing some seasonal songs. There is no deliberate effort to teach the children in any formal sense. The conscious activity of the teacher is imitated by the children.

Following the morning snack, some of the children help clear up while others go off to a second period of free play or another artistic or handicraft activity. Here the children follow by example and may paint or model for as long as their interest lasts. This might be the time to go outdoors into the garden or sandpit, or may even involve a walk to a nearby park. Once more everyone returns, coats and scarves are hung up, things are carefully put away and then all gather, perhaps around a chair in the 'story corner.' The morning concludes with the kindergarten teacher telling a fairy story. By then the parents are waiting outside to collect the children. Some kindergartens include afternoon sessions as well. In this case lunch is eaten, followed by a rest and then further periods of play.

Each day of the week has its own artistic or handicraft activity, such as a baking day. While most kindergartens offer water colour painting and drawing with wax crayons, or beeswax modelling and eurythmy, the handicrafts vary according to the facilities or the particular skills of the adults concerned. In all these activities the children learn by example, finding their way in to the experiences at their own pace. In this way the children learn to explore and be creative whilst acquiring a love of work. This manifests itself in an increasing mood of self-reliance and calm industriousness when the children are engaged. The same mood is carried over into creative play. A strong and lively rhythm helps give the children a deep sense of security.

Nimble fingers and nimble minds

In the Steiner Waldorf kindergarten the emphasis is on children mastering physical skills rather than abstract intellectual ones. On the principle that nimble fingers make nimble minds, which modern neurological research has borne out, children are helped to awaken into their bodies and especially the hands and fingers. As the neurophysiologist Professor Matti Bergstrom of Helsinki University put it:

> The brain discovers what the fingers explore ... If we don't use our fingers, if in childhood we become 'finger-blind,' the rich network of nerves is impoverished — which represents a huge loss to the brain and thwarts the individual's all-round development ... If we neglect to develop and train our children's fingers and the creative form-building capacity of the hand muscles, then we neglect to develop their understanding of the unity of things; we thwart their aesthetic and creative powers. Those who shaped our age-old traditions always understood this. But today Western civilization, an information-obsessed society that overvalues science and undervalues true worth, has forgotten it all. We are 'value-damaged.[5]

By learning how to grasp and manipulate in a meaningful way with the hands, a functional basis is formed in the child's mind for the later development of 'grasping' the world through concepts.

By modelling their behaviour on those around them, children acquire skills in the same way that they acquire their mother tongue, not by being taught but through imitation combined with the unfolding of innate interest-driven formative forces. The learning environment is wholly integrated rather than compartmentalized and subject based. This is achieved by the 'natural' homely atmosphere of the kindergarten. The development of mathematical, conceptual or coordination skills arises experientially out of the practical activities, such as those described above. Language skills are strengthened through children being encouraged to speak freely and describe their experiences. Listening is equally important to the cultivation of language skills and this is encouraged through oral story telling and listening to each other. The recitation of rhymes, counting verses and poems, carefully chosen for their language content, strengthens

sound and especially syllable recognition, an important precondition for good literacy skills. Emphasizing oral skills
also helps the children extend their vocabulary and develop
their powers of memory. Speech training forms an important part of the training and subsequent in-service development of the kindergarten staff. The voice is after all the
teacher's most important teaching tool.

Perhaps the most important skills learned in the Steiner
Waldorf kindergarten are social. In their creative play and
daily activities, the children learn how to relate and interact.
The kindergarten is permeated with a warm atmosphere of
care and interest for others. The adults, the kindergarten
teachers and assistants, work together as a team in a
collegial and mutually supportive way. There is a close
connection to the parents and, since most kindergartens are
part of a larger school, there is a strong sense of community
and continuity as the older brothers and sisters move up the
'big school.' This close sense of community is not only
supportive for the adults, it is vital for the children and
enables them to feel the kindergarten as an extension of the
home.

There is a strong emphasis on caring for the environment. The kindergarten children are daily involved in this
and sometimes the older pupils come to help in the garden
or to build a play house. The parents, too, often come in at
the weekends and in the holidays to decorate and do repairs,
and of course they are often there for parents' evenings. All
this strengthens the children's sense that people are helping
each other, working together and tackling the problems that
arise. If this is the natural social environment which
children associate with community, it can only strengthen
their sense of security and confidence. They will learn soon
enough that this is not always the way of the world. Let
them experience a hopeful archetype first so they can later
find the inner resources they will then need.

4. The heart of childhood

Kieran is quite an individual and yet in many ways typical for his age. Beneath the mop of auburn hair his freckled face has lost the puppy fat it had a year ago when he was in Class 4. Now at the age of eleven his whole figure, like his face, has become lean, even wiry. His chest and shoulders are not broad like his older brother's nor are his arms and legs muscular, in fact his prominent knee joints make his thighs seem quite skinny. But he is strong and above all agile. Watching Kieran effortlessly climb over rather than open the gate, leap onto his mountain bike and, standing on the pedals, jump the bike off the kerb and onto the road, I am struck by the unselfconscious ease of his movements.

Like most children in Class 5, Kieran has left childhood behind but has not yet entered into puberty. This age has rightfully been called 'the heart of childhood.' In the fifth class the children are eleven years old. At this age the children are typically characterized by a particular harmony, mobility and enthusiasm for life. This age represents a high point in the development of the archetypal qualities we associate with childhood such as openness, enthusiasm, playful ability, vigour and flexibility. In the years that lie ahead each individual will make their journey into puberty, a descent into matter, weight and the disorientation that comes with the emergence of a self-conscious inner life. At eleven most children have gained a mastery of their bodies through the schooling of their life forces and they have gained a new relationship to themselves and their surroundings through the crisis of identity that comes around the ninth and tenth years.

That is not to say that all children at this age are happy and well-balanced. Their individual destinies will have

coloured their experiences. Their social circumstances will
have helped or hindered their sense of being at ease with
the world. But whatever their personal development has
been, most children, like Kieran, will have individually
achieved a point of stability and harmony which is a kind
of culmination of their childhood, a high plateau reached
before the difficult descent into puberty. It will be many
years before they reach such equilibrium again.

Kieran was a round-faced, dreamy child in kindergarten.
At first he had clung to his mother, which had somewhat
embarrassed her since her older two had felt at home from
the first day. But he soon settled in. He was always most
comfortable in the group when stories were being told.
When it came to entering Class 1 he showed a marked
reluctance to leaving the familiar world of the kindergarten.
His older brother and sister had raced ahead with their
writing and reading, almost faster than the progress of their
classes, but Kieran showed little interest in letters and
preferred to draw pictures or play.

His parents began to worry when Kieran's older sister
made typically blunt comments about his lack of ability.
The mother spoke to the class teacher who was reassuring
to the mother but somewhat puzzled herself. She was aware
that Kieran was not really focused on forming the letters, let
alone reading. His drawings were still naive, large figures
floating on the page, awash with vibrant colour. His letter
drawing remained loose. He was clearly only dimly aware
that the symbols represented sounds that could be combined
to form words. When the whole class recited their numbers
and tables he joined in with enthusiasm but on his own he
lacked any clarity and just grinned, revealing that he had
lost his front milk teeth but the second ones had not yet
come down.

The class teacher had discussed Kieran with the other
subject teachers who taught the class. It was apparent that
he enjoyed joining in during both the French and German
lessons, heartily speaking the verses and singing along.
None of the teachers were particularly concerned about him
as he seemed to be very much socially integrated into the

The Tower of Babel (Class 3 drawing)

class, was cheerful and took part in everything. But the class teacher was worried that the parents' concern and the teasing of the older sister might put Kieran under pressure and spoil his enjoyment of going to school.

Following a home visit and a frank chat with both parents, all parties felt more reassured. The father took the view that Kieran should take as long as he liked to learn how to read, the mother undertook to speak to the older sister who was eleven at the time. As it turned out the sister had taken to reading to Kieran at bed time and in a very matter of fact way began pointing to certain words in the book and getting her younger brother to repeat the word. I don't know if this helped Kieran learn to read but it certainly helped with the teasing.

At the end of the first term in Class 2 Kieran missed several weeks of school due to a painful ear infection. He

Tending the class garden

Working on the farm (Class 3 drawing)

was very upset at missing the class Christmas Play. After a fairly miserable Christmas holidays Kieran returned to school. About three days into the first week the class teacher noticed that Kieran was cheerfully and fluently reading to his desk neighbour. It often happens that a development in one realm of a child's life releases block-ages in other, apparently unrelated areas. It is the task of the educator to try to see the whole child. Sometimes nature provides the stimulus for change, sometimes we have to provide opportunities by creating learning situations.

In Class 3, during the summer term when Kieran was nine, there was an incident in the playground when Kieran was rude to another teacher and then ran away. This was something of a surprise to all concerned. Although he later apologized (having been asked to do so) he actually seemed quite cheerful about the trouble he had caused. It was not long before he had become a real handful, usually in the company of a group of children from his class. They adopted the habit of stealing the other children's ball during

Hard work on the farm

playtime. The games teacher was the first to tackle this new social dynamic and introduced some new games involving groups of 'naughty elves' who had to steal 'treasure' from the giant's garden. If caught, they were 'stuck in the mud.' This challenge to the giant's authority seemed to both delight the children and at the same put the activity into a framework of rules which contained and formed the tendency, which in the playground was becoming a nuisance.

This kind of challenge to authority is typical at this age and marks an important stage in emerging self-consciousness in the child. By feeling part of a group who are asserting their identity the individuals themselves have an experience of asserting themselves. To explore the reaction of the rest of the world and in particular the responsible adults, is partly why they do it. They want to test the strength of the bond of authority that stretches between the individual, or in this case group, and the law-giving representatives of society itself. By pulling on and stretching this bond, they not only want to test its strength but gain a sense of self-will in the process. As educators we must respond with comprehension and at the same time clarity of purpose.

Teachers must set the rules of social behaviour and make them visible and tangible or else the children cannot learn them.

To help this process the teachers in Class 3, when the children reach this significant moment of development, tell the children the narratives of the Old Testament. In mythological form the story of the Creation, the Fall and the subsequent history of the Hebrew people mirrors the stages of the emergent personality and the community of personalities. When the human being is no longer in direct communion with the realm of divine origin, that is in individual terms when self-consciousness in the child arises, laws must be given so that the people may have guidance. These laws are given via the prophets. They determine how social and moral life are to be structured, they give form and context. But the people invariably stray, individuals test the parameters of divine influence, they are proud, head-strong, even downright defiant and rebel against the jealous, angry God Jehovah. At this particular stage in child development such myths are rich in soul-nourishment.

Coming to terms with earthly responsibilities and tasks is also very much appropriate to this age. For that reason the class teacher explains how food is produced on the farm, how animals are cared for, how houses are built and how the division of specialist workers is necessary. In these topics and in many others throughout the Class 3 curriculum, the children are given opportunity to find themselves through direct experience or through the awakening of their imagination.

Around that time, when Kieran was nine, he informed his older brother on the way to school one morning that he was going to become a farmer even though it meant a lot of hard work. His reason for this decision was because he wanted to drive a John 'Dread' tractor. When his brother corrected him to 'John Deere,' Kieran retorted indignantly that his class teacher Mrs Derby had said it was 'Dread.' His insistence on the authority of his class teacher impressed his brother who also knew the correct name of the make of tractor. Kieran himself was uncertain and had evoked his class teacher's name in the hope of winning the argument. Wisely the older brother backed down with a conciliatory 'Why don't you ask her?' Kieran did and Mrs Derby confirmed the make of tractor. When confronted by his brother, who wanted to know the outcome, Kieran proudly admitted his mistake but added 'Mrs Derby said that John Dread would be a good name for a tractor anyway.'

Authority does not mean authoritarian. It means being clear about what is right but also providing what the situation requires. The teacher had corrected Kieran but given him a way forward. Each time a child runs up against unyielding authority that is sterile, doors of development are closed. If mistakes are only ever wrong, where is the incentive to try again, let alone learn from the mistake. If each setback is experienced as defeat there can be no hope. Too many children are turned in on themselves, demoral-

Viking longboats

ized or simply down trodden when they get it wrong, as they are bound to do. On the other hand, if every error or folly is tolerated, if adults give in to children's every demand, then they will not develop the enthusiasm to learn. Enthusiasm is the fuel of the will, the will to learn, to have a go, to try again, to progress. Such will is awakened through encountering the right kind of authority.

In Class 4 Kieran loved the stories of the Norse Gods but increasingly complained at home that his class mates were stupid and that school was boring. He often said that he wanted to go to a proper school, meaning simply another school. He increasingly fell out with his brother and sister. A crucial moment occurred when he forgot his lines during a class play. He was struck dumb and went bright red in the face. This trauma was quickly reversed when his classmates on either side of him — he was one of the warriors at Freya's feast and they were sitting on a bench wearing horned helmets — whispered his lines to him. During the camping trip which followed Kieran regained contact to his friends in the class. They had a great time, hardly slept at all and cheerfully tramped through the rain for three days exploring the surroundings. All talk of other schools was dropped.

Such minor crises of identity are the stuff of child development. Sometimes a supportive word from his class teacher helped but as often as not one or other of the activities or the content of one of the many stories took hold of him and put him back on his feet. That goes for all children. The curriculum is so rich and attuned to the developmental needs of the children that each child sometime finds some aspect of what they do or what they hear directly relevant to what they need. The wealth of narrative is so rich that each child can find a mirror to their own hopes and fears. Furthermore the children learn from each other in countless ways that cannot be pre-programmed. One can only put children in the right situations and feed them the right experiences. To do that means understanding where they are at as each life phase is different. Kieran is now eleven and feels at ease with himself and the world.

Drama production

He is willing and able to learn, in fact he is hungry for experience. But he does not want pre-digested fare, pre-packaged experiences. He wants to make his own connections.

The gracile bodily harmony of this age is matched by a healthy rhythmical constitution with strong powers of memory and an alert curiosity. Both of these qualities express themselves in ways which can make eleven year olds a handful for parents and teachers. Their lively interest can lead them far and wide and they can be remarkably independent and self-contained. They may prefer to spend much of their time out of doors roaming, engaged in their own imaginative creativity. They can be quick-witted, ingenious rascals, collectors of 'schoolboy' paraphernalia with bulging pockets, scuffed shoes — invariably untied — and a resistance to norms of personal hygiene, both the boys and the tomboys.

From the back, Nina could have been a boy. In fact from the front it was not much clearer. A long curtain of thick black hair swings back and forth across her upper face. Standing there among a group of boys there was little to distinguish the sexes either in dress or stance.

Nina had moved to the school in Class 3 when her mother moved from Sweden, having moved there two years previously from Spain. At that time Nina was a tiny waif of a child who hardly said a word and whose voice was so faint when she spoke that it was difficult to follow her anyway. Her parents, the mother from Chile, the father from England, had separated and she had spent a year or so passing back and forth between the parents. Now she was living with her mother who as a journalist was often away. Mother and child were living with the father's mother, who had encouraged the daughter-in-law to send the child to the Steiner School. The mother had been sceptical but was prepared to try it out and basically left the decision to Nina.

In many ways Nina was remarkably self-sufficient, she was used to being on her own and seemed to cope well. For her class teacher, however, she presented something of a mystery. She rarely said much, did what she was told but remained on the fringes of the social life of the class. Physically she remained tiny in comparison with her class mates.

Eventually, the class teacher managed to make an appointment to meet Nina's mother at her home. The meeting was somewhat fraught and there were many interruptions on the phone. What made it even more difficult was the mother's insistence that Nina be present for the discussions. In the course of the discussion the mother became very emotional and defensive and began to blame the school, the absent father, life in general and, ultimately, herself. Nina seemed unaffected and even comforted her distraught mother with a maturity unusual in a ten year old.

It became clear to Nina's class teacher that the child was not being permitted by her life circumstances simply to be a child. She was using most of her energy just maintaining her stability in an insecure world. She was starving her own

development. The teacher resolved to try and strengthen the domestic situation by encouraging the mother-in-law to take more of a maternal role at home and by encouraging Nina to make a stronger connection to her work at school and in particular to encourage her artistic work. In fact it was possible to provide some support lessons during school time during which Nina was able to release some of her tense-ness through curative eurythmy and colour exercises. During this time Nina formed quite a strong relationship to the support teacher who encouraged her during her one-to-one lessons to talk quietly about her concerns. It turned out that Nina had a lot to say that rarely if ever was able to be expressed elsewhere.

It was during the grammar main lesson that the class teacher began to see something in Nina that came from her, that expressed a different side of her wishing to emerge. Although English was not her native tongue, Nina clearly had a grasp of grammatical concepts that was way ahead of the rest of the class. Several times she volunteered (in itself a new behaviour) helpful images to express the essence, for example, of the tenses of the verbs. This was much appreci-ated by the whole class. She clearly had a vivid sense of the abstract concepts involved. In fact during the course of the three week main lesson block she became positively talkative. As the smallest in the class she took to pulling her classmates about to position them on or behind the lines drawn on the floor to represent a spatial presentation of the relationship between past, present and future. The children didn't seem to mind Nina being so bossy, in fact they seemed to enjoy her enthusiasm.

The other thing that Nina was very good at was singing in parts. The children singing her part soon learned to follow her voice when singing two or three part songs. The class teacher was soon able to depend on Nina to hold one part while she supported the children in another.

Soon Nina was part of the in-crowd in the class and was often invited to stay over the weekend with one or other of

Admiring one's work

her classmates. This was something the class teacher discretely encouraged through the parents as she felt that contact with family life would benefit Nina.

Recently in Class 5 Nina had formed a very strong attachment to the Egyptian Goddess Isis during the ancient history block when the class teacher had told the children some of the central myths of that culture. The children had all listened with rapt attention to the origins of that ancient civilization, the building of the pyramids and the stories of the Gods. They had drawn many beautiful illustrations and Nina had chosen to do a whole series of drawings in Egyptian style on the theme of Isis and Osiris. After a week or so the class teacher had moved on to Ancient Greece. Now the whole class had been somewhat reluctant to leave Egypt but they were soon enticed away by the Greek legends. Not so Nina. She was determined to finish her series of Isis drawings. She had found illustrations in the library and was engaged in a fairly ambitious artistic project. She refused to write up or illustrate any of the new material on Greece. At first the class teacher insisted she finish her Egyptian work at home and keep up with the Greek work during the lessons. This was not possible for Nina. She had by now undertaken to learn hieroglyphics from a booklet from the British Museum and was attempting to write the text in ancient Egyptian script.

Something told the class teacher that there was more to this fascination than met the eye. Nina was allowed to complete her work, or at least to continue for the time being, on condition that she made short notes on the new material. This she did with great skill. She was able to take notes with such precision that many Upper School students would have been put to shame. When the great work was finally handed in, beautifully illustrated, the class teacher sat down to read the text, fortunately written in English with a border of hieroglyphics. Nina's version of the story of Isis deviated in several key points from the version that the class teacher had herself related to the class.

Suffice it to say that Nina had reinterpreted the myth to give expression to a deep inner need in her own soul. To

Anubis and Horus (Class 5 drawing)

what extent she had consciously chosen the imagery was unclear. The more the class teacher thought about it the more apt it appeared. Of course it was not all comprehensible, but then myth deals with realms beyond rational interpretation. It was clear, however, that Nina had found a medium to express processes within her own biography, forces at work in shaping her destiny. What's more, afterwards she never showed any interest in the work but seemed happy to get on with being an eleven year old. It was as if the task had risen within her, needed fulfilling and had now resolved itself.

In retrospect the class teacher could see that in a largely unselfconscious way Nina had sought out the experiences she needed to make sense of her life situation. That is the beauty of the Waldorf curriculum. It offers a range of contents, topics, inner and outer experiences, that speak to the child at the developmental stage they have reached. Each child will respond individually of course. All will draw nourishment from the broad range of subjects and if the texture, the detail, is rich enough, individuals will find what they specifically need.

Content is by no means all there is to a curriculum. The method of presenting the curriculum is often more important. This is one of the reasons why narrative is so crucial in teaching. A good story well-told engages the children in a very special way. But equally important is making your own experiences. The art of teaching often involves leading the children to a state of receptivity through which they can make discoveries that remain as profound experiences. There is much talk of making discoveries in education today but it is a far more difficult thing to do than many people might realize. Essentially the kind of experience that counts is of a deeply personal nature. It is a kind of 'eureka' moment in which the whole of the child's being is given over to the phenomenon and strong feelings of wonder, amazement, surprise or even shock are generated which leave a lasting impression. Even more important than the initial encounter is the *ah-ha!* experience that follows when the phenomenon is grasped in its relation to what is already known. This kind of discovery is like a rediscovery, things are *re-membered,* put back into their place in the world and the world thereby derives meaning. Giving the world meaning in a way that awakens the feelings of a child is a central task of education. If a child gradually discovers that his or her own biography has meaning, if they can make sense of life through the experiences they have through school, then school work assumes a much more profound significance.

It is beyond the scope of a volume of this size to go into detail about the curriculum in each class of a Steiner Waldorf School. Chapter 6 follows the development of the environmental curriculum vertically through the school from the youngest to the oldest classes. This should give the reader a sense for the development of the curriculum in at least one of its strands. The reader is advised to turn to the recommended specialist literature for more detail on what is taught when.

5. The Upper School

A new birth

If we look back at our own adolescence we can all remem-ber a certain turbulence. In some individuals this experience is more painful than in others but nevertheless we all pass through a period of fundamental readjustment in regard to both our own individuality and our relationship to the world and people around us. Maxim Gorky graphically described this period in the third part of his autobiographical trilogy *My Universities:*

> I needed only to go out into the street for an hour or so by the gates to understand that all those cab drivers, porters, workmen, clerks, merchants didn't live in the same way as myself and that those people that I had grown to love didn't want the same thing and were not following the same path. Those people whom I respected and trusted were curiously alien and solitary, and they seemed to be outsiders among the great crowd, among filthy, cunning, toiling ants laboriously building up the hills of their lives. This kind of life struck me as stupid and deadly boring. And I often noticed that people were compassionate and loving only in what they said, in their actions they submitted to the general order of things without even noticing it. Life was now very hard for me.[6]

Rudolf Steiner described it more objectively as a period when:

> ... with puberty an element of soul is born which works outside time and space. An inner world awakens. It dashes tumultuously against the outer world. Forces that give rhythm to the body become free with sex maturity, and now manifest themselves in adolescents as a susceptibility to idealism. They now project their inner nature into the outer world. A young person in this state finds everything different from that world in which he or she lived formerly with one which is now opened to the senses. Their overwhelming desires come up against endless opposition.[7]

It is this sensitivity of feeling that at this age causes such a direct reaction to what is seen as either hypocrisy or injustice.

As we traverse this period of our lives we experience stages of personal development when our emotional, intellectual and volitional life are transformed. Observation shows that these stages are common to us all, just as is the onset of physiological maturity. With puberty human beings develop the physical potential to reproduce their own kind and this momentous new capacity heralds a new human being in ourselves. The golden years of childhood recede as the young adult emerges. All such changes include some element of pain and it is not surprising that this readjustment in the human psyche can manifest itself in symptoms that are often contradictory. A golden rule for all adults who work with young people in this age range is not to judge solely by appearances. That which is being born in both boys and girls is a new, fragile, inner self which requires the protection of an outer appearance, as a sort of mask, which can appear at times to be negative, aggressive, surly, rude, taciturn and other less amenable sides of human nature.

Here schooling has a role to play that goes beyond the mere memorizing of facts that can be poured out in an examination and then safely forgotten. A real education is that which attempts to inwardly nourish the young person and work with their inherent idealism so that they can retain a sense of purpose that, albeit subconsciously, will later manifest itself in the adult. Young people of this age are all idealists. In their view, with their awakening critical faculties and burgeoning capacities of feeling, the world should be a better place and the awareness that it is not can lead to both disappointment and frustration. This stage of personal development involves the struggle to balance the subjective and the objective — which for most of us is always difficult to attain, but in an adolescent is more pronounced and intense. If no attempt is made to resolve these questions at this age there is a real danger that a further healthy maturation into adulthood will be inhibited.

Class 10 drawing after Michelangelo

HEAD OF EZEKIEL - MICHELANGELO

Ideals

We all carry ideals within us. The basic judgment of what is right or wrong is a measure against that which we would consider to be ideal. Adults, however, can stand back from their ideals and hopefully consider their realization with equanimity and thoughtfulness. For the adolescent, on the other hand, ideals are an intrinsic part of their very nature, often felt with a zeal and passion that is difficult to recapture later in life. To make education a meaningful process for them idealism has to pervade not only that which is taught but also the structure and the relationships within a school itself. It should nevertheless be a practical idealism, not a utopian vision of the perfect social order which we cannot attain and which would remove people from the reality of everyday life. Idealism and realism need not be considered as antipathetic, nor need ideals be an excuse for undue sentimentalism. Idealism is the motivation which drives humans to better themselves and their environment. In adolescence, the gaining of such an insight can be a balance to the contradictory emotional tides of becoming an adult if they are approached with the wisdom, humility and humour of a good teacher who can engender enthusiasm and respect in the young person.

All teachers are also idealists, that is why they endeavour to teach, but this can be subjugated to their circumstances as D.H. Lawrence experienced in the early years of the twentieth century. In *The Rainbow* Ursula is his semi-autobiographical *persona* and through her he vividly depicts what tragic consequences the loss of idealism can have. Embarking on her teaching career she travels on a drizzly day on a comfortless tram through a grim and ugly nineteenth century industrial town and on her way she anticipates that it will be her ideals whereby 'the veil would be rent that hid the new world.' Arriving at a grimy and squalid building she meets her fellow teachers who are either cold and unfriendly, or evasive and insincere. They are invariably rude to each other and her classroom reminds her of a prison but she is undaunted for 'here she would realize her dream of being the beloved teacher, bringing light and joy to the children.' But it isn't long before she falls into conformity, her great ideals become ashes, and although she remains a competent and well liked teacher she nevertheless in her heart feels despair:

> Why should the children learn, and why should she teach them? It was all so much milling the wind. What folly was it that made life into this, the fulfilling of some stupid, factious duty? It was all so made up, so unnatural, the school, the sums, the grammar, the quarterly examinations, the registers — it was all a barren nothing![8]

Steiner speaks of a way of dealing with ideals so that one doesn't sink into this abyss and the way forward is to unite the ideals of art, science and religion so that together they can become 'love engendering.' We experience a duality between the natural order of things in which there are no ideals, just merely cause and effect, and the moral choices that being human implies. In the natural phenomena around us we perceive that no moral or other ideals are directly visible. On the other hand, we are painfully aware that human existence could not unfold if there were no ideals. Yet with today's consciousness one cannot always experience one's ideals in a way that makes them credible. The events of the twentieth century are readily inimical to considerations of the value of ideals and in our fragmented society we easily find ourselves prone to cynicism, scepticism or relativism. We can find within ourselves a disparity between our feelings and our values. When either working with, for example, electricity or magnetism, we cannot see our inner ideals working in the natural order of things. So on the one side we perceive the natural world, on the other side our ideals, and we cannot bridge the gap. This dichotomy is there because we cannot see the bridge. It is precisely this bridge we should be struggling to construct when we devise a curriculum. For Ursula this is

Byzantine Art

For almost 300 years after Jesus's death, Christianity survived as the faith of an oppressed minority within the Roman Empire. In 312 AD its destiny changed when Emperor Constantine became a Christian and there was a sudden need for churches. Large buildings called basilicas which were meeting places/town halls for Romans were gradually converted to become churches.

Within a few years Christianity became the official religion of the empire of all Roman Europe. Constantine founded a city to rival Rome on the site of the old Greek colony of Byzantium, where he also built the basilican church of Saint Sophia. This city was called Constantinople (Constantine's polis (city)). Constantine also gave Rome a huge basilica. There was a long argument for art in churches; some argued that allowing sculptures in churches was like the pagan idea of worshipping statues and therefore should not be allowed.

Rome said no to art in churches but the Byzantine church allowed pictures in order to tell bible stories because most people were illiterate. This decoration was mostly glass mosaics. There were also many icons in the church; their aim was not realism but a sacred way to make a link with the spiritual world. These are still used in places like Russia where they are almost identical to those used in the early Christian times.

Icon

Class 9 history of art

the mystic vision she achieves after great pain at the end of the book:

> She saw in the rainbow the earth's new architecture, the old, brittle corruption of houses and factories swept away, the world built in a living fabric of truth, fitting to the overarching heaven.[9]

Thinking and feeling

We all know that we think, but rarely consider how we arrive at our thoughts. Just as we grow physically so do our thinking capacities change as we develop and any valid curriculum has to take this into consideration. In G.B. Shaw's words schooling should be a question of 'a child pursuing knowledge not knowledge pursuing the child.'

Although these stages of development are those which all individuals pass through, they are more complex than a simple progression and cannot be fully described in a schematic form. There are, however, points of emphasis.

A sign of growing intellectual ability is the capacity to criticize and adolescents are formidable critics. Their perceptions have awakened to such a point that things are no longer simply accepted as they are, but become targets on which they can practise their growing intellectual powers. Judgments are made with a firm resolution and everything they meet is put into categories of either good or bad, 'wicked' or 'naff.' The authority that parents or teachers previously had over the child just by virtue of their vocation or position is undermined and respect has to be won again on a new basis. Provocation tests the adult world and behind such activities lies the latent question 'What are you going to do now?'

At fifteen, however, this remorseless categorization is attenuated by an acceptance that there might be grey areas between the black and white. With the realization that most things are neither entirely good nor bad a whole spectrum of possibilities open up in between, and each of these possibilities can have an existence in its own right. At this age human relationships become of paramount interest. The exuberant and sharp outer challenge of the fourteen year old becomes a more inner process and it is at this point that the stirrings of a new force begin to be felt. This is the new capacity of love. All children naturally 'love' but this love is generally felt for the immediate family and authoritative adults such as a favourite teacher or a kind friend. Around fifteen to sixteen the young person can feel love beyond these boundaries. Love can be an earth shattering experience, because the person who feels love becomes a different personality and has to come to terms with this impelling force. This is often an underestimated force in human nature when we come to consider education and where we often just regard its problematical nature. With its tremendous strength for the future the capacity to love lies at the basis of all our relationships. It is therefore somewhat bizarre that

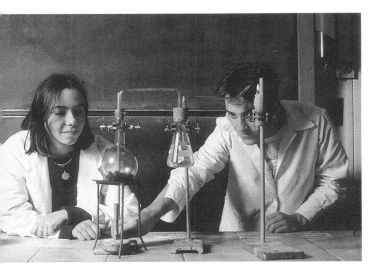

Chemistry experiment

schools are expected to exclude this feeling because it is judged to be just a part of a student's private life, without taking into account the fact that love and its associated feelings colour the young person's total view of the world and of what they learn.

At seventeen the students become, in a sense, a contemporary of the adult world. The awareness and capacities of a young person relate more to the adult world in front of them rather than the world of childhood behind them. The intellectual ability of analysis opens up their minds to that which is the prevalent thought processes of our times. However this clear analytical thinking ,that tends to atomize the world into its constituent parts, is not without its attendant feelings as well. The ability to analyse leads us to have to make choices, which means having to be for or against and either feeling emotional attachment or separation. Whereas in the young adult the quality of criticism was oriented towards the outside world, now, for the student, analysis becomes inwardly directed. 'Who am I?' 'What am I going to do in the world?' 'What am I good for?' 'What am I going to do next and what will my career be?' 'What are my capacities?' Seventeen year olds have a full realization of their own flaws and failures and should therefore be supported in finding their strengths. These too are points that can be worked with in a sensitive curriculum.

Going beyond this we can try in E. Schumacher's words to 'look at the world and make it whole' but not in the unconscious faculties of the very young child but now in the alert consciousness of the awakened adult. Being able to synthesize, creating new connections, forging new links, is what motivates an eighteen year old. At this stage they can look back at their childhood with an objectivity and an interest that does not make them feel they are being childish in doing so. A stage of development has been reached that can be experienced as a culmination of all that has been learnt up to this point and an added curiosity awakened to continue learning for the rest of one's life.

This has been, of necessity, a very cursory survey of adolescent development but it shows a pattern of development that enables the educator, who should also take cognizance of the fact that there are more complex developments, to create and develop an education that is both meaningful and stimulating.

In practice

Throughout the Upper School there are regular main lessons, as in the Lower School, but now it becomes impossible for an individual teacher to have enough knowledge and expertise in all the subjects that are necessary for an adolescent and therefore these lessons are taught by specialists. These specialist teachers will be with a class for their first lesson in the morning for a period of three to four weeks and after this they then move on to another class to be replaced by a colleague. In this manner an Upper

School class can experience ten or eleven main lesson blocks in a year, some of which may be devoted to practical subjects. In this way a mosaic of interdependent subjects is fashioned, each of which has its own particular discipline. That these lessons and subjects are orientated to the development of the young person is just as important as it was in the Lower School, and the presentation and timing is such that they can hold the young person's interest and enthusiasm.

A few examples will be given here and in the next chapter we will consider how subjects run vertically and horizontally throughout the whole school. Themes that were also dealt with in the Lower School can be taken up again in a form that is suitable for an adolescent and aspects are made conscious that were earlier experienced in the realm of feeling. By the age of fifteen the pupils have outgrown the authority of their class teacher. Now the need is for

Plant observations

people who are specialized in certain subjects and can supply their students with authoritative and trustworthy knowledge, which can also be questioned on a deeper level. This does not mean that each teacher only teaches one subject exclusively; they will teach within a certain range of subjects depending on their training, background and interest. The continual care of the class will be in the hands of one of these colleagues, referred to as either the sponsor or the guardian, who will have a responsibility for the pastoral care of the class and this colleague will have to ensure that all the teachers connected to the class are working as a team. Many schools have adopted the practice of having one sponsor lesson a week so that students do not get neglected and the pulse of the class can be taken on a regular basis. This task, however, is not straightforward for what an adolescent brings into the school community can have a divisive influence on those around them and the discrepancies between the needs of the individual and the complex demands of those working with them have to be reconciled.

Class 9

In a Class 9 the humanities main lessons could include: modern history, history of art and history of drama, and the sciences could be: human biology, organic chemistry, mechanics, maths, geometry and physical geography. This would vary a little from school to school, and country to country, but there would be a similar basic pattern in all schools. We will here take history of art as an example. This is a main lesson that is particularly effective in Class 9 and if it is taught either earlier or later its impact is diminished. In these lessons the students trace the history of western art from ancient Egypt to the Renaissance. The students themselves would be expected to produce a main lesson book containing their own copies of the art they have seen and written essays either of interpretation or fact.

Through these exercises they develop their abilities of perception and they experience that there are many ways of looking at a human being none of which is more correct than the other and, more demandingly, they will put these perceptions into a written form. They discover that the yardstick of beauty has evolved over the ages and each culture has considered different motives art-worthy. They will also discern that what at first sight would appear as art of the past has an immediate relevance to our contemporary life, in that it can depict elements of the social context, the feeling of individuals and the ideals of the human spirit in a way which still lives with us.

When they were younger children they themselves experienced the oneness and continuity of the world striven for in Egyptian art with its sense of timelessness and of humanity being guided by benign authority. With Greece they can follow their sense of burgeoning rights, a new concept of freedom and an ability and wish to take decisions for oneself. When looking at Roman art they can see that it strives towards naturalism, where people look as they would do externally in everyday life but have somehow lost the spark of youth and idealism that was there in Greek art. They are depicted as complete individuals who are also careworn, sad, aged or are portrayed as an allegory of virtue and valour. The underground catacombs of Rome show a regeneration of art in a new age. The skills and luxuriousness of the art on the surface are put aside for a simpler form and for those who understand and know these pictures they tell stories of hope, promise and rebirth.

The students will then consider the mosaics of Byzantium and Ravenna where the figure of Christ assumes that of an emperor and judge and the golden background speaks of a heavenly realm removed from this earth. In the Renaissance they note the emergence of linear perspective, physical realism and a heightened sense of individualism, but this time with an enthusiasm and a sense of potential for humanity as an explorer of the world through science. In Italy, however, art remained ideal in that the true reality of pain and suffering was still avoided. When they then survey

Computer instruction

northern European art they see humanity depicted with all its tragedy and everyday concerns even in an ostensibly religious picture. This main lesson could then culminate with Rembrandt, in whose pictures darkness becomes a force in its own right, yet light has the power to illuminate and shine upon the individual bringing a sense of warm humanity and awe.

Experiencing art in this form is not readily forgotten. It speaks directly to the ideals and latent questions of an adolescent and helps them consider the world of moral behaviour and human values without any didactic preaching from adults. Polarities of colour and form, light and darkness, idealism and reality, the struggle for achievement and the potential of inborn facilities, are both the content and experience of the lesson. It takes on a deeper and wider context than just studying art. They are exploring the realm of human consciousness and its feeling for the aesthetic by various means, such at looking and observing pictures and statues reproduced as slides or in books, studying artists' biographies and discussing differing opinions of the works in question. These themes can then be taken up later again in either Class 11 or 12 starting with the study of neo-classical and romantic artists and then through the art of the nineteenth and twentieth centuries.

In the physics main lesson one can take into account that the young people, being in tune with their own times, wish to be considered as the citizens of the earth and here they are helped to see that just as technology is the product of the human mind so it, too, can be understood and controlled by human thinking capacities. The world of en-gineering, technology and science is a reflection of our-selves and all the forces that are used in the machines around us are also actually contained within us. This block will usually start with the explanation of the development of the steam engine and pumps and how these were used to create mechanisms that brought revolutions to our cultures. The students will study the laws of dynamics and then look at the principles behind turbines, heat exchangers, radio-activity and electronics. Then they will learn to understand how telephones, electric motors, generators, internal com-bustion engines, televisions and nuclear fusion work and how they affect our lives. This is placed in the context of the inventors and pioneers themselves with their failures and successes, as well as their approval or dismissal by the general community. Humanity wins new powers and at the same time new responsibilities. Behind each machine are a person's striving and ideals now produced in a material and functional form. Like art they have their intrinsic beauty and the pupils will be expected to work and produce main lesson books that show a respect for others and their own accomplishments.

As well as what has been experienced in the above two main lessons, just two out of the ten or eleven in the course of this year, the students will be expected to follow a programme that might superficially look similar to that of other schools but yet tries to be in accord with the basic philosophy of Steiner Waldorf education. Craftwork is

Potter at work

Upper School building project

regularly practised and is particularly important at this stage where the activity of the body should not be disregarded, that something of beauty can be created and a sense of achievement enhanced. There will be regular lessons in the modern languages, maths, the native language, religious studies, and usually a period of general sciences with an introduction to laboratory techniques and practices. Gym, games and Eurythmy will follow their course in the Upper School with undiminished importance, so that although the final exams are coming ever closer the whole human being is still exercised and learning.

Class 10

Casting a glance at Class 10 we can take a literature main lesson as an example, where the subject is seen as an arte-fact of our culture with its depiction of skill and motivation, together with the human connection to the earth and the all powerful feeling of love in its many transformations. In Europe this main lesson could take the form of a study of the classical story of *Odysseus* who was forced to go 'in search of his own soul' during his long and much delayed return from Troy. His suffering and adventures are part of an inner struggle in which he eventually succeeds through the power of his mind and by the image of Penelope's faithful devotion at home. His agility of thought and cunning prowess allow him to escape the most threatening of situations to become the protégé of the Goddess Athena who was seen by the Greeks as inspiring and reigning over the human mind.

The Teutonic stories of the *Volsunga saga* or *Niebelung-enlied* show a much harsher environment, where men and women alike are expected to follow a severe code of honour regardless of personal feelings. Duty, kinship, the posses-sion of land and position are the highest virtues rarely mitigated by any tenderer feelings. Revenge is required even if darkness and personal despair ensue. Love however is triumphant in the Celtic stories of *Tristan and Isolde* where recklessness and even disloyalty become necessary if the forces of the heart are to be the guide for human conduct. Tragedy does ensue but it is a fate that shows the immortality of love and its ability to transform our lives. These three themes not only show aspects of all human feeling life but are also the strands that provide the founda-tion for the historical development of the Middle Ages, which is again taken up in Class 11. In this way world literature is not just read but is also experienced as uncover-ing aspects of our intricate and sometimes contradictory nature.

This mixture of thought, feeling and activity is also to be

found in the surveying main lesson usually taught in this Class. Here the pupils are given the task of surveying a particular landscape and reducing it to a representational map. This will not only need scientific accuracy and mathematical skills to translate it to paper but also mutual co-operation and sharing of tasks. The natural world is observed and catalogued but the pupils gain an astonishing revelation that what at first sight seems a small patch of ground contains an enormous variety and is never the same from one day to the next. Out of all their individual efforts a map is constructed and their sense of achievement is augmented by it being something useful. Performing a full length play is also a way of consciously learning about the interaction between the individual and the larger group at this age. It is a potent lesson on how it is possible to pull together in a situation that by its very nature exacerbates tension and finally something praiseworthy and artistic is produced and appreciated, in spite of all the practical difficulties, nervous strain and concomitant fraught relationships in the class and the teacher

At this point, at least in the United Kingdom, the students are well into their examination work at this stage and this requires a difficult compromise for the school. The examinations must be done as well as possible so that students are at no disadvantage in the choice of their further vocation and, in fact, in most cases the results are very good. However they do necessitate a lessening of main lesson work and in some situations a complete cessation of a Waldorf approach in exam lessons themselves in favour of the syllabus as laid down by the examination board. Some schools make this compromise less painful by taking the examinations a year later i.e. in Class 11 and Class 13, which has proved very much to the pupils advantage, in that they have been able simultaneously to keep their interest and enthusiasm in the main lesson as well as coping with the exams. This added year of maturity has proved to be an advantage in many respects. However, in an ideal educational environment a comprehensive and full Waldorf approach throughout the Upper School would be preferable.

Classes 11 and 12

One of the central main-lessons in Class 11 is that devoted to the medieval tale of *Parzival* as written down at the beginning of the thirteenth century by Wolfram von Eschenbach. It tells the story of a young man who in search of the Holy Grail suffers much and passes from innocent stupidity, through doubt to eventual blessedness. It is a long and complex book but all students readily appreciate it because it is their story; it is a story of their own inner evolution that they recognize. Although set in medieval garb it is strikingly contemporary, dealing as it does with questions of material affluence and spiritual values, ambition, inherited characteristics, freedom, renunciation, doubt, despair, the conflict between pride and humility, redemption and forgiveness. There are often heated debates on questions of guilt and innocence, in how far we are responsible for our fellow human beings of whose existence we might not even be aware, about our guardianship of the earth, the relationship between men and women, cultural and religious diversity and self-knowledge. At seventeen all these are existential questions and many ex-scholars remember this main-lesson with particular clarity.

Parzival is born into a royal household but from the beginning has to take on the failings of his father, Gahmuret. He had been a restless individual who could find his home neither in Arab kingdoms of the Middle East nor in his native realm of Anjou. Although he had all the outward trappings of success — wealth, good looks, power, fame and a beautiful and accomplished wife — he could find no satisfaction in these and eventually got himself killed in an unnecessary quest. Herzeloyde, his wife, is determined that her son will not be drawn into his father's footsteps and brings him up as a naïve fool in the depths of the forest far removed from the knightly culture of the court. But when Parzival is sixteen he comes across some of King Arthur's knights and immediately decides he wants to become one as well. In spite of his mother's protestations he leaves her for the wide world without any preparation for what he will find there, to the extent of not yet knowing his own name and identity. Through his ignorance he brings grief to many and in the process unfairly kills a cousin of his in a joust in order to obtain his armour which he believes will make him a real knight. When after many mistakes he gains wisdom and compassion he finds he is inwardly driven to remedy his previous mistakes although this path leads him to great despair and nihilism. He learns that all humanity is born to take responsibility for others and if we cause harm, however unwittingly, this becomes something we then have to carry. Through sheer determination, loyalty and deep love he is able to redeem himself, find his rightful place and is then blessed with the capacity to help others. These exploits are a mirror for the young person in which they can explore their own principles and guiding ideals.

In Class 12 the teacher is working with young adults and they must be respected as such. The nature of the lessons should change and be much more of a dialogue than hitherto, with less need for the formalized work habits of the previous years which have already been established. Here all the threads come together and the lessons are so constructed to overarch any narrow subject boundaries. Architecture is the final aesthetics main lesson. It is the art we cannot do without, whenever we build we create it and it reveals us for what we are. Our buildings are an outer image of how we feel as we inhabit our bodies and it expresses our thought patterns, our ability to deal with the material world, the moods of our soul, our sense of direction and our social mores. Following its evolution over the last five thousand years enables the student to see the enormous variety of human life with its unfathomable complexities and diversity, yet its oneness in a common striving for something better. One can compare across ages, say, an Egyptian pyramid with a skyscraper, a Somalian mud-hut with a Gothic cathedral, and find them of equal value as evidence of the human predicament. Architecture contains all the arts and is a product of all human senses. It effects us continually, even if subconsciously, and the world is in turn influenced by its practice. For eighteen year olds it is like reading an exciting new language, the language of human evolution and ideals.

It will probably come as a surprise to realize that what was described above as the main lesson programme is actually only one fifth of what is actually taught in main lessons in these four years. The object is that there is no untoward specialization and that all facets of human endeavour and understanding are found to be fascinating. Although the Waldorf programme itself finishes in Class 12 many schools add an extra Class 13 solely for the exam study, where the young people are in an environment similar to any further education college to enable them to concentrate on this last remaining challenge before leaving school.

Through the Upper School there has also been a craft curriculum that runs from copperwork and forgework in

Diary of a class exchange

Sunday 9th May

We went for a lovely cycle trip along the Danube, then by the Ille, (Mums other river). We swam in the Ille and had some lovely sausages which we cooked in a fire. We all became red and hot because it was such a hot day. We cycled home, and on the way back we bought some delicious ice-cream (Malaga it was called).

Class 9, to bookbinding and papermaking in Class 10, jewellery and silverwork in Class 11 and sculpture in Class 12 to name but a few possibilities. In painting and art they have continued to use different methods, styles and techniques. Drama and music are as equally important and by the end of an Upper School each student will be familiar and able to deal with Information Technology and all the necessities of daily life. They will have also experienced trips to theatres and museums, camps, field trips, class exchanges abroad for a period of a few weeks, working together with less privileged people, work experience and a cultural trip abroad.

All these children are indeed fortunate that their parents have chosen this form of education for them but we are convinced that such an approach is what all adolescents should receive by right. By teaching them through ideals one can supply a rich fare which they can experience with enthusiasm and will help them over the hurdles of growing up. What happens after school is less easy to collate. However, it does seem to be the case that they all go into different paths as adaptable, fulfilled and continually developing adults.

6. Environmental education

The ecology of childhood

Perhaps one of the most important tasks of education in our times is to establish a healthy relationship to nature. A true sensitivity for the environment has to start in early childhood. Mankind has become separated from the natural world and this remains true even if many of us feel committed to the environmental cause. Having a bad conscience is one thing, actually taking on active responsibility or even exercising stewardship of the environment, is quite another.

Merely knowing that nature needs to be respected is not enough. This knowledge must permeate our will, it must become part of a healthy common sense and this is something that children can learn much better than adults. Children can feel a part of the natural cycle of the seasons, can identify with the plants and animals in their own environment, and are gradually able to learn that people have a responsibility towards the natural world.

When children are young it is so much easier to learn that there are things that need doing at particular times and that there are things that we just don't do at any time. Mere concepts mean little to them without direct experience. Later they can learn in detail why things are as they are. If they learn how natural it is that everything is inter-related, that one thing influences another and especially that nature is animate and possesses *being,* as they do, then it is much easier to acquire a scientific, ecological understanding once the faculties of abstract thinking and judgment have developed.

If we expose unprepared children to the idea that people are destructive and are responsible for the pollution of the air, the waters and the soil, there is a danger that children will lose the trust they bring with them that the world is good and filled with meaning. That can lead to alienation and insecurity in adolescence or later. Nor should we give our children romantic pictures of a sentimental world that has never existed. Children are quite capable of understanding and accepting the mysteries of death and decay as long as these experiences can be placed within a context they can relate to. To find and bury a dead bird in the garden with an appropriate word or two has meaning to a young child, as does the knowledge that grandfather has left this world and is with the angels. What we tell the children is not as important as whether it has real meaning for us. The child draws security from knowing that we know. It is not a sentimental world that children need because that would be

Baking in the kindergarten

fundamentally superficial and unreal. What children need to encounter is the real world explained by adults they trust in simple, but not simplistic, terms they can understand. This means neither abstract, scientific concepts nor baby talk, but concrete images drawn from the world they are familiar with.

There are also, of course, things that can't be explained but that is also part of growing up. There is also the anticipation of being told 'You'll learn about that when you are in Class Eight.' Or even better for older children, 'The reason for that has not yet been discovered.' Now that is a challenge that is hard to resist. It is exciting to know that there are still some things to be done in life!

From the whole to the parts

How then do Steiner Waldorf Schools actually tackle environmental issues? The fundamental lesson children have to learn is that *they need the world and that the world needs them.* Naturally this can't be done entirely in the first class. Nor can it be merely communicated as an abstract fact. It is a recognition one grows towards through many experiences. In fact the whole curriculum offers opportunities to experience the qualities of nature and to grasp the fundamental principles of ecology.

The Steiner Waldorf method of teaching is in itself ecological in that it starts from an assumption of the whole and then seeks to understand the parts within the context of the whole. From the first class onwards this method is developed throughout the curriculum. In the earliest introduction of the numbers we proceed from the division of the original unity, the oneness, to the duality, from there to the trinity and so on, staying initially with graspable numerical values familiar to the children. 'What is there only one of?' the teacher asks the children. From one sun, one moon and one earth the child discovers that there is only one *me,* and the magic of that is that it is true for everybody. In this children have a consciousness of number similar to that of pre-industrial peoples who experienced number qualitatively as well as quantitatively. As Steiner put it:

> Counting began from unity. Two was not an
> external repetition of unity but it lay within unity.
> One gave us two and two is contained in the one ...
> It was (in earlier times) an inner organic picture
> where two came out of unity and this two was
> contained in the one, likewise three and so on.
> Unity encompassed everything and the numbers
> were organic divisions of the unity.[10]

In the introduction of the letters one goes from a tangible whole to a symbolic part in that the shape of the letters are abstracted from a picture by discovery. The children find the letter H in the teacher's drawing of a house. Likewise, reading begins with the recognition of a written line that the children already know by heart. Only gradually is the child's consciousness drawn to the recognition of individual words. Later, when grammar is taught around the age of nine, the spoken sentence as a whole and complete entity is analysed to discover *doing words,* names, subjects, objects and indirect objects by asking who gave what to whom? Thus real relationships are established before their syntactical structures are identified. Sentences are taken literally, with children acting out the 'parts.' The tenses of verbs are grasped through their spatial relationships in time: before, after etc. Simple and progressive verb forms are understood as describing different states of being; I eat but at the moment I am speaking. Passive and active verb forms speak for themselves but in indirect speech, someone speaks for you and tells you what they said, or allegedly said, or would have said if ... and so on. Understanding language in this concrete way is always to place it in a context the child can identify with.

When this approach is done in an artistic, creative way then the relationship of the parts to the whole is a living one, in which the whole expresses more than the sum of the parts and the identity of the parts is complemented by the

A nature walk

whole. The mood that this approach creates, and it can be applied to other activities, not only numbers and language, far better reflects the reality of ecological relationships within the living world. To introduce concepts remote from their context and the real experience of the children, is akin to the reductionist building-block approach which inevitably must remain one-sided and partial. As long as the child's comprehension of a phenomenon is open to enhancement through subsequent experience, then the foundation for a holistic understanding of organic processes has been cultivated. Fixed, additive forms of knowledge, or rather information, are inappropriate to understanding the living world.

The young child

The very young child does not experience the same distance and separation from the world as the adult does. The consciousness of the child is much more focused in the world around them. Young children especially can devote incredible powers of attention to their focus of interest, they are absorbed in what they are doing. One need only observe a young child watching a squirrel in the park, or bluetits pecking at a bag of nuts, to see how strongly they identify with the object of their interest. The child experiences the animal's movements and gestures right into his or her limbs.

The same intensity of experience is poured into play. There the child driving a truck (actually a block of wood in adult terms) around the living room carpet is wholly given over to the reality of the imagination. The close link between the imaginative faculties and the world of nature is never more apparent than in young children. Close observation of children shows that they are less concerned with outer aspects of nature and certainly don't see the same things as an amateur ornithologist when watching birds. What children experience appears to be much more in the realm of movement and gesture and what one can only

Ploughing

Scrumptious apples

describe as mood. Children are very sensitive to the atmosphere of place, a damp, dark hollow in the earth, a wide stretch of shining wet sand, a snowy forest. They do not remember the outer detail and can scarcely describe it, but they know how it felt. Whenever children have an intense experience of natural phenomena, say a cold wind, a frightening dog, stinging nettles, a moon hiding behind the clouds, what lives on in their memories are complex vivid pictures bound up with the child's own feelings and reactions. Such pictures are common to the language of fairy tales in which the natural world often takes personified form, with elemental beings inhabiting the different realms of earth, air, water and so on. Here, too, we hear of the whispering wind, the laughing waters of the stream, the wise old owl. These 'soul-pictures' may be short-lived in terms of the child's actual memory and active vocabulary, but they remain long in the sub-conscious, providing a background tone to many subsequent experiences in life.

If the child's attention is drawn to such natural phenomena by a familiar and trusted adult and these experiences are put into an imaginative context, they may be a source of joy for life. Some leading naturalists, professors of biology, such as E.O. Wilson and Stephen Jay Gould, both of Harvard, have each noted that childhood wonder was the source of their lifelong interest in nature. (The passionate interest of these two great scientists has not prevented them from fundamentally disagreeing with each other's theories!) The same source of wonder has been noted by many poets and writers. Often an adult, perhaps a grandfather, has introduced the child to the magic of nature and sown a seed that grew and flourished throughout a lifetime. To be told on those special occasions when the sky is filled with sunlight and rain that the fairies are baking, explains nothing in adult terms but creates an indelible mood of magic. To be told that the rainbow is caused by light refracting through raindrops is neither plausible to a child nor particularly inspiring.

Causal explanations and biological science have their place of course and can also be a source of wonder and amazement, but only when the child's own cognitive faculties are capable of understanding the context. This comes later. At first, with parents and in kindergarten, a more fundamental relationship to nature and the natural rhythms of the seasons needs to be established. And this is done primarily through direct experience, through taking walks in wind and rain, sun and cloud, singing songs, collecting natural treasures for the nature table, using natural materials in play and above all celebrating whatever seasonal round of festivals is appropriate to the region. One does not need to live in idyllic rustic surroundings to do this, nature is everywhere, even on the urban wastelands. In some places we might just have to try a bit harder, as adults, to relate to nature and thus be able to guide the children.

Nature study

This mood of wonder needs to be transformed into active interest. In the kindergarten and the first school classes the children are embedded in a 'natural' world through the seasonal festivals, nature stories and the like. Towards the age of nine they need to have their interest increasingly guided in a more conscious way. At an age when children begin to experience a stronger sense of self and a corresponding sense of distance to those around them, it is time to learn how humankind gets to grips with nature.

Children need to learn how our shelter and nourishment depends on the transformation of natural materials and that this process implies a special relationship between humankind and nature. The children learn that with the gift of nature's bounty comes the covenant of responsibility and stewardship. The children of Class 3 experience this through the powerful mythic pictures of the Book of Genesis in the Old Testament, in which a cosmic and holistic vision of the creation is given. These images are imbued with a mood of reverence and respect for the whole of creation. In archetypal form the children experience how mankind learned how to till the soil and build communities.

During the same school year the children learn about real farming. They experience how the farmer has to work with and even constrain the forces of nature, weeding the crops, building fences, protecting the lambs, draining the land, getting in the corn before it rains. It is important that the children have direct experience of the work and many classes not only visit a farm but spend time picking potatoes, raking up hay or whatever suitable tasks can be found. Where possible children can sow a patch of corn, tend it and harvest it in the school garden and then, having milled the grain, bake bread and eat it. In the same way during the house building main lesson, the children learn how raw materials are transformed and used in building. As well as visiting a building site, it is usual for the class to undertake some building project, often involving brick-laying, to make a garden wall, or a brick oven or a playhouse for the kindergarten. Whatever it is, the work must have a real function and be made with real materials.

Laying bricks

People and animals

In the fourth class, ten year olds begin their first zoology lessons. The theme running through these lessons is that animals are what humans have. Various classes of animals are described though a typical example and their specialized adaptations to their habitat and way of life are characterized. These superb though one-sided adaptations are compared with human abilities, the gnawing teeth of the mouse, the wool of the sheep, the wings of the bird. The animal's physiology and activity are compared with that of our own, showing the animal's expertise and human limitations. However, the freedom available to the human being through bipedal uprightness and 'unspecialized fore-limbs' becomes very apparent to the children through the comparison when they take into account the technical achievements of humanity.

In this way the children become aware of the unique role the human being has in relation to the animals and can gain a feeling for the universality of human nature. In order to fully grasp this the children have first to form a strong identification with the animals being studied and be able to marvel at their skills and prowess. This depends to a large extent on the teacher's descriptive powers which are crucial in engaging the children's emotions. They must be able to slip into the animal's skin, as it were, to really bring the qualities alive. The children then give expression to their feelings towards the various animals in drawings, paintings and even poetry.

Botany

While of course the study of animals continues over the following school years to include lesser known animal groups and the world of insects, in the fifth class plant life takes a special place in the curriculum. In the botany main lesson the plant world is treated as a whole living organism.

Plants are not isolated as specimens but seen as integrated in their whole environmental context. In describing the typical plants of the different landscapes within our own region, and later the various geographical regions of the earth, or the changing biotopes from sea-shore to alpine meadow, the children develop a living sense for ecological thinking itself.

Animals speak to children in a more immediate way. To discover the nature of the plant world a different, more patient mood is required. Botany is studied through two essential media, observation of life and imaginative description. Both methods are interdependent. Without first having described the nature of particular plants, be they flowers, fungi or trees, the children may have difficulty seeing their qualities in nature. If they already have an inner imaginative picture then each encounter with the plant in nature has the character of a discovery. If they only see images or reproductions, or isolated specimens, they will never grasp that the nature of the plant can only be grasped in context in the living world.

To start by dissecting plants into their parts or to examine a specimen in the classroom, far away from its mossy bank or light-speckled clearing in the beech woods, is to misunderstand the nature of plants. The introduction to botany is vital in establishing a conscious recognition of ecological realities. In the botany main lesson the children learn to recognize how familiar plants, such as the dandelion, vary in shape and size according to the soil and light conditions they grow in. The class can be taken out into the school grounds, a local park or into the country to find and describe dandelions in their various environments. They are often amazed at the variety it is possible to find in even a small area, from large plants with broad light-green leaves growing in good soil and full light to small dark plants with narrow, strongly indented leaves forcing their way up between the paving stones or in the cracks of an old wall. The same exercise can be down with common trees such as the sycamore or elder.

The children can soon learn to identify the various parts

and organs of flowering plants. The stages of development of the growing plant can be observed with quick growing annuals and the growth phases can be related to the seasonal qualities. Here simple techniques using window boxes or small beds in the school garden can suffice to engage the children's attention.

Once such principles have been discovered the children can then learn about plants in different regions other than their own. They can, for example, draw the progression of plant types from the salt marshes around a river estuary, back up-stream through flood meadows, on up into the uplands and finally to mountainous alpine plants. A comparable imaginative journey can be made from tropical regions up through Mediterranean climates, through temperate zones on up to the tundra and taiga. If the teacher has the knowledge, one can also show the range of plants in a rain forest from floor to canopy. In this way a wonderfully

A landscape painting

living picture of plant life in relation to the environment can be given.

One of Steiner's indications on how botany can be taught was to find a relationship between the plant world and the children's own understanding of themselves. Just as the different animal types can be understood in the fourth class as one-sided developments of archetypal human abilities, so too a correspondence can be found to the plants. This cannot be done at the level of activity. Plants, unlike animals, are not what humans have. The three-fold nature of the human being, with nerve-sense, rhythmical and metabolic-limb systems finds an inverted relation to the environment in plants. In the limb system, the human being is at its most interactive with the environment. This quality belongs to the flowering, fruiting and reproductive processes in plants which are most sensitive to the surrounding light, air and warmth realms. The seed has, of course the greatest capacity to 'move' in these elements. The rhythmical expansion and contraction of the leaves and branches up the stem of flowing plants corresponds to the human rhythmical system and the vertical rising and falling of the sap is analogous to the fluid systems of the human body. The plant root, contained within the dark, cool earth with its complex balance of micro-organisms and mineral qualities together with the spherical tendency of its form, correspond to the head. In this sense we have an inversion, a plant with its 'head' in the ground.

But there are other, more psychological, analogies. This is not to suggest that plants have a psychological life within them. Far from it. Lacking a central nervous system, the plant has no inner, let alone representational or emotional life. But plants in their colours and forms, in their relationship to their environment, in their whole being express qualities which we can personify or characterize in psychological terms. This is not to anthropomorphize but rather to show that certain soul qualities exist as archetypes and come internally to expression in animals to some extent and consciously in humans to a greater extent, and which plants express outwardly.

A landscape sketch

Plants express a certain character or mood, whether it be the shimmering delicateness of the aspen, the gnarled defiance of the oak, the tall brooding remoteness of a Douglas fir or the generosity of the broad chestnut. Flowers, too, have their character: the broad rustic face of the sunflower, the fluttering butterfly transience of the poppy — so beloved of Impressionist painters — the rich luxuriance of a full blown rose. The flower language of the soul has a long and noble pedigree in the history of art. Fungi too have their provocative shapes and sickly and sometimes lurid colours and earthy smells. Such qualities of trees and fungi and flowers, including of course their scents and perfumes, their herbal and medicinal properties, awaken an inner life of feeling in the children. A year later, in Class 6, the pupils will already be too self-conscious and pragmatic for such delicate and ephemeral soul pictures. In Class 6 they need minerals, rocks and precious stones with qualities measured on the hardness scale.

While much can be done in the classroom, there is no substitute for field trips carried out in the locality. By observing how common plants such as the dandelion vary in different soils and different conditions of light and shade, in a crack in the pavement or among the vegetables in good garden soil, the children can gain some fundamental experience in understanding the organic world.

In our age of media culture, children often have a short attention span. When nature, for many children, means grand spectacular scenery and dramatic landscape, it can be difficult to interest them in the small, the local aspects of their environment. When outdoor activities mean extreme pursuits like white-water canoeing or rock climbing, pitting oneself against the elements, having the latest hi-tech survival equipment, simply going for a walk in the park or nearby woods may seem tame. As a result it is necessary to engage children in active work. Merely looking is not enough. Without a grasp of the small things, such as the role of the earth worm, near to hand, many children's relationship to nature will remain superficial and sensational.

Real work

At the age of around twelve, with the onset of puberty, the pupils need to develop a more physical and practical relationship to the earth. It is in Class 6 therefore that gardening lessons begin. Of course the children are no strangers to the school garden. They have been regular visitors since the kindergarten. They may have sown and harvested corn in Class 3. Now, however, they have for the first time the physical strength to really do the physical labour necessary for gardening. Even that is doubtful for many of them. Many children today lead such relatively sedentary lives that an hour's strenuous work in the garden is too much for many of them. Nevertheless, a certain division of labour between those who can and those who can't usually sees the work done.

Quite apart from the physical aspects of the work,

gardening is a precise science and the children learn to make observations, collect seeds, make compost and work out rotation plans. Gardening creates a special awareness of causality in a living context. If we don't weed the peas they will be overgrown. Too much water can be as bad as not enough. There is a wonderful natural logic to work on the land. Time is a key factor for the young adolescent to come to terms with. Naturally the seasons bring their appropriate tasks but perhaps more significantly the pupils learn that things happen in their absence. It is different in woodwork. When you leave your piece of joinery over the vacation, when you come back it is in exactly the same state as when you last saw it. In the garden things can change from one lesson to the next.

Gardening also helps the pupils gain practical insight into the economic aspects of production. They can calculate how much the seeds cost, perhaps even the water, but they discover that you cannot put a price on the soil and air, or indeed on their efforts as gardeners. When they come to price their produce, perhaps to sell in the school shop, or at the Christmas Fair, they learn that finding the right price for their herbs, flowers, preserves and so on, is a complex business. Apart from anything else, the children gain a healthy respect for food producers in the economy. They look at the supermarket shelves with new eyes once they too have some experience as producers.

The mineral world

At this age, too, the pupils are able for the first time to really grasp the influence of the mineral world on geography and human activity. As strong mineralization processes begin in their own growing bones they also have the cognitive skills to grasp the laws of the inorganic world. Geology is also an introduction to basic chemistry. Essentially though, the rocks are studied for their influence on the landscape. The pupils explore, for example, what a limestone environment is like, what plants grow there and what

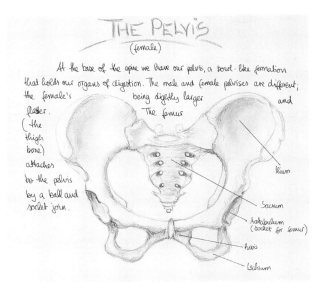

Drawing of pelvis

kind of economic activities it supports. Steiner placed great
emphasis on the typology of rocks and minerals in this age,
and experience has certainly shown that geology is always
a popular subject in Class 6 or 7. It has something to do
with the young adolescent's wish to stand on solid ground,
understand basic facts about the world and there is little
more basic than bedrock!

Classes 5, 6 and 7 see the laying of a broad foundation
in botany, mineralogy and soil studies combined with
practical gardening. The link between these closely related
subjects is self-explanatory. In Class 7 we return once more
to the human being and in particular human biology. The
link to the natural world is found through the theme of
health and nutrition, both of which have a strong connection
to the environment. What we take into our bodies relates to
our health and also to illness. Plants play a particular role
in both our health and nutrition. With puberty comes a

strongly egotistic attitude to health, physical appearance and fitness. It is good to cover the basics of 'what is good for you' at an age just before this narcissism becomes too acute. It is also a good time to relate to 'what is bad for you' which also has to do with nutrition and substance abuse.

The pupils learn about the digestive processes, about how their bodies metabolize and regenerate (sleep is often a topic) and also about how we nourish ourselves through the senses. Discussion of respiration and digestion leads to a description of the main illnesses of these systems, which in turn leads to the use of healing plants and minerals. This is also a good age to address questions of responsibility, morality and personal freedom in relation to health. The pupils are now old enough to discuss the question of instincts and drives and the question of self-control, particularly in relation to sexual behaviour.

The Upper School

Class 8 marks the end of the class teacher period in which the main morning lessons are taught by the class teacher. From now on the blocks are taught by specialist teachers who rotate every three or four weeks. The change from being taught by an all-rounder, a generalist, to being taught by subject specialists means a significant shift of emphasis in the teaching method. Whilst the class teacher was able to speak with the confidence of a well-informed enthusiast, the Upper School teacher places the subject itself in the foreground. The experiences speak for themselves, the methodology lies in the nature of the subject matter.

Things are not quite as simple as that, though the trend lies clearly in that direction. From the age of fourteen onwards the individual undergoes such a major transformation that we are justified in referring to this as the end of childhood. Steiner referred to this age by coining a very apt term (in German, *Erdenreife*) best translated as 'earth maturity.' Puberty is a kind of maturation of the earthly side of the human being. With the characteristic growth spurt that accompanies puberty comes full sexual maturity and a noticeable experience of bodily heaviness in total contrast to the effortless mobility of, say, eleven year olds.

Far-reaching, new psychological dimensions open up, bringing with them much inner turmoil. Many young people experience a profound loss of orientation during this period of their lives, particularly with regard to friendships and relationships. There is often such dissonance between physiological development and the emotional life that deep crisis ensues. From the point of view of our theme, the consequences can be withdrawal from the environment and a rejection of the young person's own organism. Extremes can manifest themselves in such conditions as anorexia and bulimia.

The educational task at this age is to accompany this maturational process in a healing, integrating way. Human biology plays a key role, in particular those organs which relate most closely to the outer physical laws in their organization and function, the sense organs, the skeleton and muscle systems. Later the questions of reproduction and embryology are worked with both from a biological point of view but also from a personal and emotional side. Birth is discussed, often by a mid-wife who has been invited as a guest, as are the moral issues of abortion. Then, in Class 11, one can discuss early child development, language acquisition and parenting. At that age the students are sensitive enough to understand the issues, whilst finding ample scope for their blossoming idealism. Most seventeen year olds profess themselves to be (potentially) sensible and responsible parents, an attitude that probably goes some way to ensuring that it will be some years yet before they actively consider parenthood. It should be stressed that we are speaking of co-educational classes of mixed ability students and not advanced level biology students.

In very brief outline the Upper School biology and environmental science curriculum covers in human biology the organ systems related to the senses and comparative anatomy and ecology as a subject in its own right, usually in

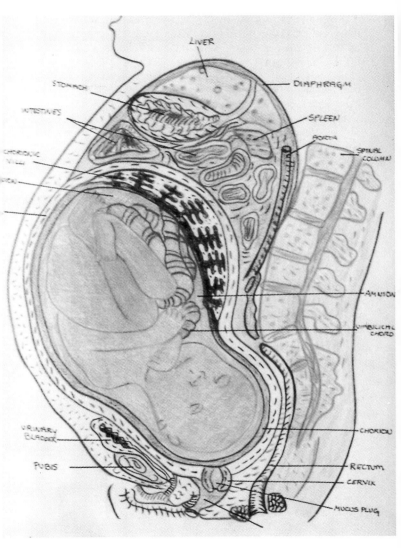

Drawing of an embryo

connection with field studies. In Class 10 in human biology, the inner organs are studied not only in their morphological aspects but also in their psychosomatic influences, including the heart and circulation, respiration, digestion and especially the nervous system and brain with particular focus on the nature of perception and consciousness. This more theoretical work is balanced with first aid and health and safety courses.

Environmental work plays a large role in the practical work experience blocks that come in Classes 9 and 10. There is often a three week farming and forestry practical during which students work alone or in groups on farms under the supervision of the professionals. Sometimes this is combined with surveying, an activity in which precision measurement is combined with observation of the landscape.

With the emancipation of independent thinking that occurs around the age of seventeen the young people begin to emerge from their shells more and can relate in a more flexible way to their social and natural environment. This enables them on the one hand to open themselves more to the needs of others, especially those in need of special care, the elderly, disabled and handicapped. Work experience opportunities are provided to respond to this new maturity. On the other hand, in terms of biology it becomes possible to deal with such complex issues as the origins of life, cell theory, transitions between plant and animal and the cycles of matter and energy in ecosystems, genetics and questions of individuality in nature. By the end of the twelfth class the students will have had the opportunity to study human evolution and such ethical questions as genetic engineering and human intervention in evolution, question which require a philosophical as well as scientific approach.

What started out with the young child being lead into a naive encounter with nature through story and festival, through play and direct experience, has arrived at a complex ecological understanding of the essential unity of natural phenomena. A holistic attitude has been cultivated, though one not less scientific for being so. Wonder has turned to lively enquiry, which has become knowledge with responsibility towards the natural world.

From the number of Steiner Waldorf pupils who have gone to contribute to the biological sciences, to environment work, to holistic medicine at the highest levels and with considerable public recognition, it would be fair to say that Steiner Waldorf education has made and continues to make a more than significant contribution to one of the most crucial areas of human endeavour. These are not back-to-nature eccentrics but people who make a difference because of their professional skills and insight, not to mention that best known of 'Waldorf traits' — an articulate gift of the gab! Many are at the forefront of holistic theory and practice, helping to tip the heavily weighted scales of academic and governmental prejudice away from the mechanistic-reductionist view.

7. Teaching is learning

Parents and teachers together

A school is a community and although its task and *raison
d'être* is to work educationally with the child it is nevertheless a community that also consists of adults. This statement
may appear to be a truism but if considered properly it has
profound implications. All adults connected to the processes
of childhood, whether as parents, professional teachers,
administrators, support staff or academic researchers, are,
essentially, educators. Although not everybody is directly
concerned with the curriculum as such their activities,
abilities, in-put and attitudes are part of the pedagogical
impulse of the school.

In a Waldorf School it is considered to be of paramount
importance that the parents have a close relationship to the
educational practice and an appreciation of the underlying
philosophical approach. This does not mean that an adher-
ence to the ideas is necessarily expected, rather that there is
a continuity of approach both within the school and at
home. Without this the child could easily have the feeling
of being pulled in two directions and counteractive tension
is created. To this end mutual feedback between parents and
teachers is encouraged through regular attendance at termly
parents' evenings, home visits and the many opportunities
for a quiet conversation that present themselves during life
in a school community. Such meetings need not only occur
when there is a crisis to discuss. Sharing the achievements
is as important as showing concern. The children, as well as
the teachers, feel that they have not received the support
they require if this is neglected. In these times of social

isolation the teacher is often the only caring adult parents can turn to in time of need to help understand their children and discuss how parental authority can be fruitfully exercised.

Parents play a vital role in ensuring the survival and growth of the school and this can take the form of participating in fund raising, helping with the care and maintenance of the school environment, being involved in outreach and public relationships, representing the school in the wider community, at conferences and so on. Parents will be called on to help with many school activities, plays, outings and celebrations. Such support can become a formal responsibility. Parents work on school administrative committees and become members of the school's Council of Management, the equivalent of being school governors. Many parents continue to carry such responsibilities even after their children have left. As charities, Steiner Waldorf Schools are very dependent on the good will of the parental body. Apart from these practical and administrative responsibilities, schools need the involvement of the parents on another level. School communities need people to care and caring means showing an interest, getting involved as well as giving constructive, critical feedback. Gone are the days when parents were expected to drop their children at the gates and leave everything to the professionals. Steiner Waldorf Schools were the pioneers of parental involvement. Steiner spoke of the vital role of parents' evenings and parental input generally:

> At least once a month, at any rate periodically, we try to arrange evenings when the parents of the children at the school come together ... to meet the teachers in order that a link can be made with the children's home life. We set great store by this understanding for the child's school life on the part of the parents.[11]

None of this is compulsory, in the conventional sense, but active participation enhances the children's educational experience in that they will then have the strong impression that this is a place to which they belong and which has an important value attached to it by the adults in their immediate environment. This feeling of warm support is educationally beneficial. There must at least be a ready and clear channel of mutual communication between the teachers and the parents. Many parents have over the years commented on how much they have learnt in this role both from the children bringing home the content of their lessons and also through belonging to a learning community in its broadest sense.

A learning community serving the child

In a lecture Steiner gave in 1921 entitled *The Fundamentals of Education,* where he gave a basic outline of the principles behind the new school, he said:

> However paradoxical it might sound, the child is the teacher *par excellence* in the Waldorf School. For Waldorf teachers are fully convinced that what they meet in their children, week by week, year by year, is the outer manifestation of divine and spiritual beings who have come down to earth from a purely soul and spiritual existence in order to evolve in a physical body on earth between birth and death.[12]

This awareness brings attention to the fact that it is through the children that the school exists at all and it is they who have really made the decision to be there. The rest of us are there to support this choice and make it fruitful. It also highlights the task of the teacher in that the child must be inwardly approached with reverence. 'From the daily revelations of this mysterious spirit and soul existence, they discover what they as teachers must do with their children.' Being a Waldorf teacher is thus a very demanding and also a very nourishing vocation. Nothing stands still and it becomes a part of one's daily task to try to perceive the realities behind outer appearance and to work with them creatively. However, to do this with any hope of success requires as a precondition the insights, positive approach, observations and ideas of the other colleagues and adults in the school.

In place of the head teacher Steiner, when establishing the first Waldorf School in Stuttgart, replaced this function with the collective work of the teachers on deepening an understanding of the nature of the human being. This alternative to the kind of departmental administration found to this day in practically all other schools is little short of revolutionary. It is an increasingly relevant challenge for those in education. This approach anticipates how people will need to work in many walks of life in the future. In some progressive areas of business management and organizational planning, such ideas are beginning to find increasing application. Steiner Waldorf Schools around the world have practised this form of self-administration for over seventy years.

Teachers' meeting

This daunting task requires the school to have an organizational structure that enables such research to be practised and supported. Hence the formation of what is known as the College of Teachers or Faculty. This group of teachers will generally meet on a Thursday evening. The role of the College of Teachers is to carry responsibility for the education in the school. This includes appointing and deploying staff, research and developing the curriculum, evaluating the educational provision, formulating educational policies and administering the daily life of the school; in short, taking collective responsibility for the matters usually in the hands of a head teacher, school director and deputy head. However, there is no hierarchy and all decisions are reached by consensus.

It is a challenging and demanding way to work and requires a high level of individual responsibility. To achieve this the individuals in the circle have to be prepared to constantly examine themselves, for without this willingness, and human nature being what it is, such high aspirations are likely to founder. This is a form of continual teacher training and one in which all the practicalities of running a school have to be dealt with alongside the philosophical and pedagogical aspects.

As educators we have to learn to deal with our prejudices, to examine our capacity for courage and honesty, to make the effort to really listen to what is being said, to practise imagination and foresight and, often the most troublesome, to take decisions. When this works it is not only the result of the meeting itself but also the consequence of each individual considering the matters thoughtfully in the course of the week, diligent study of the philosophy on which the school is founded, and having the perspicacity to comprehend what the children have been telling us in multifarious ways during the lessons. The children in the care of the school are aware of this inner work on the part of the teachers without having to be directly told of it, as it percolates the atmosphere around them, to which all children are highly sensitive. In this manner the whole question of human values is approached, not as the result of preconceived and immovable dogmas to which everybody is expected to adhere but rather as a field of individual and collective work. To do this the teachers will look to forces that are beyond the individual for a source of strength and inspiration.

The absence of a hierarchical structure also ensures that successful and skilful teachers are not promoted out of the classroom into a bureaucratic or managerial position. Their only ambition can be to become even better teachers and this is to the direct benefit of the child. Experienced teachers become of course increasingly involved in supporting and mentoring new colleagues and in contributing to the process of teacher training. This does not draw them out of the classroom but rather adds another dimension to their teaching.

Members of the College are usually teachers or administrators who have worked in the school for at least a year and feel themselves to be committed to the ideals and life of the institution and are also prepared to shoulder the responsibility this involves. It is therefore far less likely that one lone individual can set the tone and direction of the school. The leadership is a shared responsibility in which the aim is to draw forth talents that might even be unsuspected. This allows an element of continuity to coexist with the possibility of responding to any challenges that present themselves. For all members of staff there is a weekly staff or pedagogical meeting at which individual children or whole class groups are considered and where discussions about the curriculum are held. Items of common concern will be shared and preparations made for events or festivals in the week ahead. To help develop a greater sensibility for community, staff will also work together artistically, which also brings another dimension into the considerations than just the theoretical. In addition, there will be regular inter-faculty meetings for class teachers, upper-school teachers or for specialist groups such as those involved in modern languages or learning support. All in all, great emphasis is given to working together in order to improve all facets of school life.

Meeting and working together in this intensive way is intended to enable a conscious assumption of responsibility and simultaneously create a 'heart organ' for the school. Just as a class of children is changed by the addition or subtraction of one child, so the spirit of the school is created by mutual co-operation of everybody involved.

Exploring values

The schools in the UK and Ireland receive no state support whatsoever, unlike the majority of European countries, yet they are all determined not to become institutions that are only accessible to the affluent. Obtaining a broad social mix is a basic principle for the work. It is generally considered desirable that we should live in a tolerant and compassionate society and the foundation for this ever being achieved is laid in the attitudes we develop in childhood. If social awareness rather than class or ethnic division is to be achieved, then school classes need to consist of children of many abilities and social contexts so that the pupils can learn that everyone has an equal value regardless of their circumstances, gender, ethnic or religious background. The result of this policy is that Steiner Waldorf Schools have to struggle with being seriously under-funded and both parents and teachers alike have to make significant financial sacrifices. This is not an ideal state of affairs and Steiner Waldorf Schools would be better able to flourish in Britain if this was rectified. On the other hand this constant struggle to make ends meet is a useful palliative against complacency and ensures that a mood of mutual support is pervasive. Poverty and self-sacrifice are, however, not essential preconditions of idealism.

Mutual support and concern is a gesture towards each other and the world that has the potential to enable the teacher to discover hitherto unsuspected strengths. This is a parallel to a good teacher's approach to teaching and to the individual children in a class. The children learn most

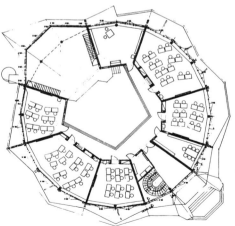

Reutlingen Waldorf School, Germany

from the unspoken gesture with which the teacher relates to the subject and to them. Values are implicit in what teachers do whether acknowledged or not:

> Chemistry can be taught in myriad ways, but however it is taught, the teacher will always be giving directions, explaining, demonstrating, checking, adjudicating, motivating, reprimanding, in all these activities displaying the manner that marks him or her as morally developed or not. Teachers who understand their impact as moral educators take their manner quite seriously. They understand that they cannot expect honesty without being honest, or generosity without being generous or diligence without themselves being diligent. Just as we understand teachers must engage in critical thinking with the students if they expect students to think critically in their presence, they must exemplify moral principles and virtues in order to elicit them from the students.[13]

A path to this end, that is expected of all Steiner Waldorf teachers, is a willingness to work on their own meditative life. This can take the form of placing in one's mind's eye the pupils who are going to be taught the next day before starting the preparation of the lessons. In this way the pupils are considered as individuals and in the task of remembering what they wore, their mood, interests and work during the day, a closer and clearer conception is built up of what they will need in the next lesson. At the same time such non-judgmental thoughts about other people has a potential of facilitating relationships and overcoming difficulties if taken into sleep. Many who have practised this experience it as enlivening and as making the actual teaching more productive. Steiner also gave meditative exercises that teachers can use to develop a greater awareness of their own personalities and to strengthen their relationships to others and the world. Through these quiet moments of reflection they can work on themselves and their capacities. It is also common practice to start important meetings, such as a College meeting, with a common verse so that in sharing thoughts the participants are drawn together in a common purpose.

Each lesson is prepared by the teacher anew, taking into account the particular class, the integration possibilities with other subjects or simply the desire to take a new angle on unfamiliar material. The idea is that the teacher will adapt the material to suit different classes. This is one of the reasons that Steiner Waldorf Schools do not teach from textbooks as they do not allow that degree of flexibility. The effort required to grasp and then to teach something which is unfamiliar can give rise to a sense of discovery and warm enthusiasm. For the children this experience is palpable and in turn it assists them in retaining their natural curiosity and zeal to learn. For the teachers new vistas are opened up and they do not then find themselves merely repeating year after year things they had learnt during their own education and training. If the world becomes an object of continual interest and engagement for them a similar gesture will animate the children.

Inner work works

Good teaching, therefore, comes as much from the heart as from the head and this has to be developed like other human skills. The republic of teachers is not an utopian ideal with little bearing on the reality of the world but rather a form that engenders growth in the adult and consequently the child. Steiner often draws the parallel between this attitude to teaching and the myth of Prometheus. In bringing fire to humanity he enkindles something that until then had been in the province of the gods and it is this gift that enables man to develop independent thought and freedom. Knowledge imbued with warmth, however hard won, is of greater value than that found in the confines of cold tradition. We do not have any real notion of what sort of world the children we are bringing up will have to face nor of the problems that will confront them in the future. The pace of technological change constantly accelerates and where this will lead us is unimaginable. We cannot just assume that the wisdom we wish to impart will be of any practical value in the future and as educators it is important we can acknowledge this and recognize the futility of trying to turn future generations into replicas of ourselves with similar views and abilities. What we can impart, however, is an attitude to knowledge and learning in which the challenge of its acquisition is life enhancing and generates genuine enthusiasm for our social and natural environment — a form of 'moral ecology.' Life-long learning is not only a question of accumulating knowledge but is based on the ability to learn from experience. That faculty is established in childhood.

It was the American philosopher Ralph Waldo Emerson (1803–82) who proposed a concept for education that stands in stark contrast to the goal orientated linear form that is so prevalent today:

> Our life is an apprenticeship to the truth that around
> every circle another can be drawn; there is no end
> in nature (this symbolizing) the Unattainable, the
> flying Perfect, around which the hands of man can
> never meet.[14]

For an adult, just as with a child, the self is paradoxically both attained and unattained. In perceiving education as a circular gesture we can become aware of an outer space that is not circumscribed by what we know and into which we can still grow. But in entering this space we become aware of yet another circle that surrounds us and so, like the flowing ripples on a water surface, we are within a process of continual growth. We can never claim to be complete. This is the gesture of an embrace which then cares for what is learnt, whether intellectually, emotionally or socially, and yet never assumes that there is no more to explore and discover.

We do not wish to suggest that Steiner Waldorf Schools are havens of co-operation and social harmony. Like all institutions they have their areas of strength and weakness that need close scrutiny and consideration. No community can expect to last for ever and of necessity undergoes a process of continual change. A school working on such principles can readily slip into an insular existence and begin to take on the trappings of an enclosed order which ultimately does the children a disservice. When this happens processes are necessary that bring about a reinvigoration so that the children receive an education that has a genuine relationship to the contemporary world. In his initial address to the teachers in the first Waldorf School Steiner referred to this endeavour:

> We dare not simply be educators; we must be
> people of culture in the highest sense of the word.
> We must have a living interest in everything
> happening today, otherwise we will be bad teachers
> for this school.[15]

This too is an inner attitude and the adults in the school community must strive together to attain a balance between self absorption and a dogmatic approach to the educational philosophy on one hand, and on the other a sensitivity to how it is viewed from outside that consequently demands unjustified compromises and hollow claims. The statement that teaching is self-education has ramifications for the whole community and its simplicity masks a plethora of difficulties and possibilities that we are just beginning to grasp.

8. Origins and future outlook

The beginning

Rudolf Steiner was born in Kraljevic, then part of Hungary, now in Croatia, in humble circumstances. He graduated at the Technical University in Vienna and later received his doctorate in Philosophy from Rostock University. Steiner was a writer who published over 30 books and gave over 6,000 lectures most of which have subsequently been published in several hundred volumes. His career as a journalist, educator, scientist, lecturer, artist and architect had by 1919 also earned him an international reputation. He was the founder of the Anthroposophical Society, which is based on a modern spiritual scientific understanding of the human being and the world. Today he is regarded as one of the leading thinkers of modern times for his contribution to spiritual and cultural renewal, philosophy, medicine, agriculture and, perhaps most influentially, education.

Barely a year after the end of the First World War, with central Europe on the brink of revolution, with the economy in ruins, political fragmentation and social breakdown, the Waldorf School was born. The industrialist and owner of the Waldorf Astoria factory, Emil Molt, asked Rudolf Steiner if it would be possible to found a school for the workers of his factory. Both men were at the time active in a political movement inspired by Steiner's ideas on social reform.

At this distance in time it is difficult to realize how perilous the situation was in central Europe. A generation had lost its ideals and millions of its young men in a disastrous war caused essentially by the inability of the ruling political systems to control the burgeoning capitalist and imperialist economies or to prevent the Great Powers from colliding. The pre-war era of progress and optimism had come to an end. The industrialized working classes of Europe had been both brutalized by their working and living conditions and partly emancipated by half-hearted political reform to expect their rights to be respected. Yet the ruling classes of the various European cultures, whether British, French, German or Russian — to name only the dominant societies — seemed still to be bound to a rigid class system and paternalistic attitudes. There were crassly extreme ideologies competing for ascendancy. On the Left, Bolshevism, on the Right a complex mixture of populist and reactionary nationalism and free-trade Capitalism. The liberal centre was weak, as indeed were the institutions charged with governing an increasingly unmanageable situation. In 1919 it could have gone a number of ways. We know that the German Weimar Republic that emerged out of the crisis was fatally flawed and the pendulum of power gradually swung in the direction of National Socialism.

Rudolf Steiner actively stepped into this disastrous situation by publishing a widely read book on social reform, known in English translation as *Towards Social Renewal,* and followed this up by addressing large political gatherings of workers, trades union representatives and industrialists. In 1917, as the war ground slowly to its conclusion, Steiner had sought to influence the course of the eventual peace by circulating a document which warned against many of the ideas embodied in the Treaty of Versailles in which the victors imposed conditions on Germany which ultimately allowed the rise of Hitler and the Nazis. Steiner argued that it would be a mistake for Europe and the world to see Germany as solely responsible for the war and therefore deserving of crushing humiliation in defeat. There were factors such as international military-industrial interests as well as political incompetence to take into account. The German nation had suffered enough and further punishment would only create political extremism. Steiner also made reference to a number of important political and social reforms.

Rudolf Steiner   *Emil Molt*

Though the document was read by high ranking military figures and members of the government, it did not, unfortunately, alter the course of history.

In the crisis of 1919, Steiner became the focus for a popular movement which became known as the Movement for the Threefold Social Order *(Bewegung für Dreigliederung)*. There is not space here to go into detail about the history and ideas of this movement. Let it suffice to say that it was motivated by Steiner's concept of a threefold membering of the social organism. This saw the three fundamental areas of social tasks: the spiritual or cultural sphere, the sphere of rights, and the sphere of economics as coexisting alongside each other in mutual interdependence but each working according to its own functional principles. The guiding principle of cultural life should be freedom, that of the sphere of rights should be equality and in economics the ruling principle should be mutual help or fraternity. These functional social principles — freedom, equality, fraternity — if applied within their own sphere can have a healthy effect on the development of the social organism. Applied in an inappropriate way, they can and usually do lead to disharmony and social conflict in the long run. The principle of unrestricted freedom in economics, for example, can only lead to injustice and conflict as recent developments demonstrate. To apply the principle of equality in a one-sided way in the cultural or spiritual life is to impose uniformity and deny individual freedom of choice or expression. Fraternity, if overdone, can be paternalistic or even, if taken to extremes, lead to collectivism and the suppression of individual development. Naturally a healthy social life requires a dynamic and conscious balance of these functioning principles.

Many initiatives were taken under the banner of the Movement for a Threefold Social Order, including industrial co-operatives, clinics, publishing ventures, research institutes and the Waldorf School. The Waldorf School was founded out of the passionate desire to create an education that would enable the individual to become not only a balanced and healthy person but one capable of making a meaningful and socially responsible contribution to society. The Waldorf School's founders had the question of social renewal very much in mind not only when the curriculum was created but also when the organizational structures of the school itself were being formed. Steiner also made it very clear in his addresses to parents that they too had an important role in the school. In a speech to parents he began by saying:

> In this school more than in any other, we need to
> work with the parents in a relationship of trust if we
> want to move forward in the right way. Our
> teachers absolutely depend on finding this
> relationship of trust with the children's parents,
> since our school is fundamentally based on spiritual
> freedom.[16]

Steiner went on to explain what he meant by the school's spiritual approach:

> You absolutely do not need to be afraid that we are trying to make this school into one that represents a particular philosophy, or that we intend to drum any anthroposophical or other dogmas into the children. That is not what we have in mind. Anyone who says that we are trying to teach the children specifically anthroposophical convictions is not telling the truth. Rather, we are trying to develop an art of education on the basis of what Anthroposophy means to us. The 'how' of education is what we are trying to gain from our spiritual understanding. We are not trying to drum our opinions into the children, but we believe that spiritual science differs from any other science in filling the entire person, in making people skilful in all areas, but especially in their dealings with other human beings. This 'how' is what we are trying to look at, not the 'what.' The 'what' is the result of social necessities; we must apply our full interest to deriving it from a reading of what people should know and be able to do if they are to take their place in our times as good, capable individuals. The 'how,' on the other hand, *how* to teach the children something, can only result from a thorough, profound and loving understanding of the human being. This is what is meant to work and to prevail in our Waldorf School.[17]

Thus one can see that the Waldorf School in its conception and birth embodied two fundamental sets of principles, the teaching method implicit in the Waldorf curriculum and the principles of the Threefold Social Order. Wherever people strive to work with both of these sets of principles within the social context in which the school is embedded, then the spirit of the original Waldorf School is at work.

As the movement for a Threefold Social Order and many

The first Waldorf School in Stuttgart

of its ventures collapsed under increasingly violent political pressure and the economic ravages of inflation, the only institutions to survive were the Stuttgart Waldorf School and the Weleda Pharmaceutical Firm. Both survived to inspire many similar initiatives elsewhere, both in Germany and abroad. This was fortunate because when the Nazis came to power in 1933 it did not take them long to ban the Waldorf Schools and other anthroposophical institutions and persecute their co-workers and supporters.

This hiatus, of course, was not the experience of the English speaking countries where they were able to continue unmolested. However, in Britain the schools had to face historical prejudices and traditions from the start. One of the first initiatives was to start an evening and weekend school for the young girls working on the looms in the mills in Ilkeston, Derbyshire. When the first attempt was made to convert this into a school it was met with incomprehension. 'A proposal to teach young children as young as five French and German in addition to English, even though the instruction may be limited to songs and poems, strikes me as ridiculous — I expect that Miss Lewes is trying to transplant into a coal village something she has admired in Switzerland without taking into account the change in altitude. Actually it is as much as we can do to get the Ilkeston children to speak English by fourteen.' Fortunately Edith Lewes, the daughter of a well established hosiery manufacturer, was not put off by this remark of one of the inspectors of the Board of Education in 1926. She erected a small building in the factory yard where classes were given in singing, drama and eurythmy and after her death she had left enough money in her will for a school, Michael House, to eventually become established in 1934. Most of the schools founded since have had to face similar difficulties.

The suspicion that Steiner Waldorf education was a foreign import, based on a central European philosophy not particularly relevant to these islands, has taken half a century to overcome and many individuals have had to make great sacrifices to ensure the survival and growth of the schools. But these episodes do underline the fact that such a universal social impulse cannot just be directly transplanted from one culture to another. It has to find its roots in the local environment and we can now see that this is, at last, being achieved. In 1923, when Steiner was giving a course of educational lectures in Ilkley, Yorkshire, he was asked for advice on the setting up of schools. His reply was that the initiators, who happened to be four ladies, should plan for a big, modern, well established school. It should not be too small because if it was to work in England this would be seen as a weakness. It should not be amateurish and neither an imitation of a fashionable country boarding school nor should it start in a poverty stricken area, like the East End of London in those days. But it had to be a school for all children and truly comprehensive.

Such has been the endeavour ever since, and the first generation of schools had to try to tread a difficult path between these extremes. In the early decades the tendency was to accommodate themselves to the more traditional private school ethos. The schools, however, benefited from remarkable acts of generosity and devotion from teachers and friends alike. Tremendous strength of purpose and sincerity were needed to develop a distinctive pedagogy in a basically uncomprehending and sometimes unsympathetic society. It was difficult to establish schools that measured the pupils' achievement by more than just academic standards. Until the mid 1970s there were only six schools in the United Kingdom. With the 1944 Education Act establishing a polarization between full state provision and private education the Steiner Schools found themselves really belonging to neither category.

The next generation of schools deliberately attempted to redress the balance by making the education available to low income families. They tried to work with a system of contributions according to income instead of a fee structure and expected parents to give support to the school by holding fund raising activities and taking co-responsibility for the fabric of the school. This approach created great enthusiasm in spite of the lack of financial resources. With strong parental support communities were built up around the schools which experimented with new forms of administration based on a partnership between the parents and the body of teachers. The education is not seen as a commodity that can just be bought but requires shared responsibility within the threefold aspect of the school's organization.

Hartsbrook Waldorf School, Hadley, Massachusetts
Überlingen Waldrof School, Germany

Another difference was that school initiative groups were increasingly set up by parents with concerns for the education of their children, rather than by teachers which had previously been the case. These new forms also had to be responsive to the changes between the first generation of pioneering parents and those who succeeded them with different expectations of the school.

The present situation is that both generations of schools have learnt from each other and are now remarkably similar in many ways. The older schools have been much more fortunate in that the finding of a suitable home was not so traumatic. They have also been able to avoid the endless search for initial funding with which the younger schools have had to cope. For all of the schools, however, it is still a constant battle to cover running costs and there are ongoing attempts to find a more secure and fairer source of funding.

Similarly the ideal curriculum has had to be compromised to accommodate the 16+ examinations and, with the advent of the national curriculum and the pressure for early academic learning, further questions remain to be answered. Nevertheless the constant struggle gives a palpable sense of purpose and has helped create school communities of great warmth and adaptability.

Education for life

In a rapidly changing society the qualities of flexibility, self-reliance and initiative are called for. The world of work is radically changing in the industrial world as the economy shifts from having a manufacturing base to having a service based one. Future generations cannot expect to follow one profession throughout their careers as earlier generations could. Learning a trade or a particular skill is useful but it is not all that is required these days. New skills are needed and above all adaptability in the age of 'portfolio careers.' Some societies, such as large parts of North America, are already far down this road. Others will soon have to follow.

For many people not having work will be the norm for long periods of time because that is how the modern economy is structured. It does not mean that the unemployed should be deemed failures or, even worse, blamed for their plight. For those in work, the automation of much of the economy is bound to mean more leisure time. What are people to do with their time, other than endlessly consume or be entertained, which is what many governments see as the social future? The title of Neil Postman's book *Amusing Ourselves To Death* aptly describes the predicament. Humankind has not won its freedom to drown in unemployment and inactivity!

The future will demand mobility, initiative and the willingness to go on learning throughout life. People will be required, as the catch-phrase has it, to think globally and act locally. The thinking, however, is always easier than the doing. This has to be a primary objective of an education that takes the needs of individuals and society seriously. Mere intellectual knowledge, of the kind that is required to pass conventional school examinations, is obviously not enough. In a world flooded with information, facts and statistics, the most precious ability will be sound judgment. How much do current school curricula do to cultivate sound judgment?

Education for stability or change?

How then can such qualities as adaptability, creativity or even common sense be cultivated? The old concepts of education were more suitable in former times when societies were more stable and rigidly structured and national educational systems needed to take little account of international forces. Children were educated to take their appointed place in society. Each social class had its own form of education, the lower classes usually having to make do with the 'school of life' after receiving some basic instruction so that they could behave as good citizens of the state.

Sekem school in Egypt

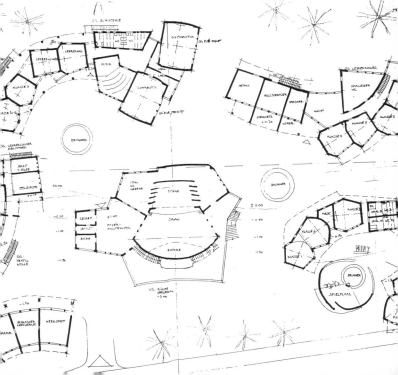

Our times need a different educational approach and there has been no shortage of suggestions. It is a feature of our times that there appears to be no one way which is right and the endemic educational reforms around the world testify to this. We live in an age where there is an expressed need for real diversity and choice. Our sense for democratic rights, however, also demands that we make such choices available to all regardless of social status or income.

The rich have always had choice, even in education. Our times demand not equality through uniformity, as earlier forms of socialism tried to impose, but equality of choice. It is the role of government to make the provision of educational choice available to all, not to determine what kind of education everyone should have, nor should it prescribe what should be taught in each lesson which, in the long run, deprofessionalizes the teacher. It may sound paradoxical and counter to the many political assumptions that until now have held sway, but it is through this choice that we will achieve the potential of creating a more integrated society. The recent events in Eastern Europe have shown that a rigidly imposed dogma and tight social control can only mask social and national rifts; when it is removed they re-emerge with added ferocity. However, when people are allowed to develop and grow in freedom and through the experience of education become aware of the obligations that mutual respect and tolerance demands, then a civic society can be created that is not based on fear but, on the contrary, can appreciate the value of diversity.

Whatever kind of education is chosen, it should take account of the needs of the developing child as well as the requirements of society. Ultimately these two priorities should coincide and there should be no conflict of interest. The recent history of educational reform in many countries has seen a shift away from the progressive child-centred principles of the seventies and a move towards educational methods deemed to be more accountable. The terminology of education has shifted to reflect the economic principles which it has been forced to adopt. In order to solve the problem of the spiralling costs of systems designed to provide universal education within the context of a welfare state, many governments have intervened to force reform. This change has usually been imposed from the top down and with little consultation. Instead of simply reforming the funding arrangements to match the strengths or weaknesses of the economy, there has been a tendency to go further and attempt to determine the quality and nature of the 'product' as well, by setting attainment targets and introducing quality controls that do not find their origin in educational practice or research.

The Philosopher's Stone of modern economic theory has cast its spell over education and the efficacious effects of market forces are expected to produce an efficient education meeting the needs of ... well, the market, of course. That such principles could be successful in education is by no means certain. And anyway how does one measure success in education? Properly speaking one can only do so by taking the whole of a person's subsequent life into account. No government could ever think that far ahead but must settle for much shorter term criteria.

Rudolf Steiner gave education a new and long term task in relation to society's needs. It radically reverses the role education had traditionally been given. He formulated this as follows:

> We shouldn't ask: what does a person need to know or be able to do in order to fit into the existing social order? Instead we should ask: what lives in each human being and what can be developed in him or her? Only then will it be possible to direct the new qualities of each emerging generation into society. Society will then become what young people, as whole human beings, make out of the existing social conditions. The new generation should not just be made to be what present society wants it to become![18]

Stavanger School, Norway

Education: the new challenge

Education has moved to the top of the political agenda. Politicians of all colours are running their flags up the mast announcing their undying concern for the well-being of the next generations, sometimes with real sincerity, at other times with acute sensitivity for the mood of the moment. It is sometimes hard to take their concern seriously. Apart from which we might ask politely, is it really the job of politicians to call for more homework or to determine the proper themes for the study of history or even which set books should be read for advanced level literature exams? Surely it is the politician's task to establish the right to a good education and provide the means. Naturally there must be a consensus as to basic standards but isn't it up to parents, teachers and educationalists to decide what constitutes a good education? The role of government and those in authority is to ensure everyone's mutual rights are respected and balanced so that no-one is inadvertently disadvantaged, not to give a legally binding prescription in great detail for a task in which they rarely have direct experience.

If politics is an art so is teaching and this artistry should be respected. It is hard won over many years, usually with great dedication, and to turn it into a playing field for political point scoring will only prove detrimental to the interests of the children.

Some commentators have suggested that politicians have realized that their traditional route to social change, control of the economy, is no longer possible in an age of multi-national companies, global free trade and financial markets that circulate the world at the speed that computers and satellites determine. Deprived of making any difference through economics, they have turned their attentions to education, which all agree does make a difference. Education has become the platform for political ideologies, a construction site for social engineering in a new guise.

Since education is about people, educational theory and practice must be based on a view of what we consider the human being to be and of course this is implicit in the imposition of a national curriculum even if it is rarely admitted. At the heart of the education debate is the question as to the nature of the human being. Even with the best will and intentions, no Minister of Education can claim to know the definitive answer to these questions which are ultimately based on self-knowledge. When governments start dictating which world view we should have it is time to ring the alarm bells of democracy! We would suggest the proper role of government is to protect the rights of children — all children — to an education that enables them to unfold their true potential and to ensure that there is proper research into all aspects of education so that good practice can be proliferated and spurious claims exposed for what they are. What kind of education that might be can only be left to parents to judge and choose allied with the insight of professional teachers and the innate wisdom of children.

A genuine pluralism and a respect for the diversity of other educational approaches is the mark of a responsible and mature liberal democracy. Government monopoly of education is obsolete in the modern world. Steiner Waldorf Schools offer a real alternative to mainstream education.

They see themselves not as competitors but as partners providing a complementary provision, contributing to and learning from other educational practice.

Steiner Waldorf is also a rapidly growing movement that spans some forty countries, many of which now publicly fund Steiner Waldorf Schools within the maintained sector. Such countries as Norway, Sweden, Denmark, Germany, Holland, New Zealand and Australia have found that having publicly funded Steiner Waldorf Schools alongside other kinds of schools with broadly comparable rights of parental access is good for pedagogical innovation and contributes to raising standards and the motivation of parents and teachers.

The schools themselves work together for mutual support in areas such as teacher education, curriculum development, publishing and commissioning of research, public relations in general as well as political and legal matters, the employment and co-ordination of advisors, the organization of conferences and exhibitions, setting up areas of discourse with other educational streams and academics and much more besides. In times of trouble, when discord can occasionally occur, Steiner Waldorf School associations are more and more proving their worth. Organizations similar to the Steiner Waldorf Schools Fellowship in the United Kingdom

Blue Mountains Waldorf School, New South Wales, Australia

are to be found in all countries where there are schools, even solitary ones. Through the work of such co-operative structures an eye can be turned to the wider world and the international nature of Waldorf education takes on a significance within the multi-cultural social environment we inhabit and at the same time be effective in the immediate local culture of the country.

As we share the globe with all its other inhabitants and have become much more conscious of our state of interdependence we should work with children in the same way and begin to dismantle the exclusive national or class system of the past. Of course the children, when young, need to be firmly rooted in the culture, language, mores and customs of their native surroundings and family, but also in the process of their own growth they have to 'branch out' and become citizens of the world which will come to meet them in ways we cannot even imagine. This mentality has to live in all those involved in a truly modern education and this is another area where Steiner Waldorf Schools can make a contribution. The seven hundred schools each respect the individuality and autonomy of the others but are also united in sharing a common philosophy that enhances the dignity of all humanity. They are conscious of their world wide embrace and see this as an added responsibility that should imbue all their work in the lessons. Naturally this is only the beginning and Steiner Waldorf Schools will evolve into something quite different, and perhaps even unrecognizable, in the future but, at least, such an attitude does look at the future, not with foreboding, but with the confidence in the ultimate good of humanity and an awareness that we have a task on this earth. This task is not only just for ourselves. It is the child in all of us that constantly reminds us of this.

References

1 Holdrege, *A Question of Genes,* Floris Books, Edinburgh, and Anthroposophic Press, New York, 1996, p.79.

2 Dawkins, 'God's Utility Function,' in *Scientific American,* November 1995.

3 *Guardian Weekend,* January 4, 1997, p.6.

4 Steiner, *The Education of the Child,* Anthroposophic Press, New York 1996, p.19.

5 Prof. Matti Bergstrom, quoted in *Paideia,* No. 11 April, 1996.

6 Gorky, *My Universities,* Penguin, Harmondsworth 1983, p.90.

7 Steiner, *Lectures to Teachers,* Anthroposophical Publishing Company, London 1923, p.85f.

8 D.H.Lawrence, *The Rainbow,* Penguin, Harmondsworth 1981, p.460.

9 *The Rainbow,* p.460.

10 Steiner, *Soul Economy and Waldorf Education,* Anthroposophic Press, New York 1986, Lecture 9.

11 Steiner, *A Modern Art of Education,* Rudolf Steiner Press, London 1972, p.209.

12 Steiner, *Waldorf Education and Anthroposophy* Vol. 1, Anthroposophic Press, New York 1995, p.101.

13 Fenstermacher, 'Some moral Considerations on Teaching as a Profession.' *The Moral Dimensions of Teaching,* Jossey-Bass, San Francisco 1990, p.134f.

14 Emerson, *Selected Essays,* Penguin, Harmondsworth 1985, p.225.

15 Steiner, *The Foundations of Human Experience,* Anthroposophic Press, New York 1996, p.31.

16 Address at parents' evening January 13, 1921 in *Rudolf Steiner in the Waldorf School,* Anthroposophic Press, New York 1996, p.64.

17 *Rudolf Steiner in the Waldorf School,* p.79.

18 Steiner, *The Renewal of the Social Organism,* Anthroposophic Press, New York 1985, p. 71.

Further reading

Books by Rudolf Steiner:

——, *Discussions with Teachers,* Anthroposophic Press, New York 1997.

——, *Education as a Force for Social Change,* Anthroposophic Press, New York 1997.

——, *Education for Adolescents,* Anthroposophic Press, New York 1996.

——, *The Education of the Child and Early Lectures on Education,* Anthroposophic Press, New York 1996.

——, *The Essentials of Education,* Anthroposophic Press, New York 1997.

——, *The Foundations of Human Experience,* Anthroposophic Press, New York 1996.

——, *The Kingdom of Childhood,* Anthroposophic Press, New York 1995.

——, *A Modern Art of Education,* Rudolf Steiner Press, London 1981.

——, *Practical Advice to Teachers,* Rudolf Steiner Press, London 1988.

——, *The Roots of Education,* Anthroposophic Press, New York 1997.

——, *Rudolf Steiner in the Waldorf School: Lectures and Conversations,* Anthroposophic Press, New York 1996.

——, *Soul Economy and Waldorf Education,* Anthroposophic Press, New York 1986.

——, *The Spirit of the Waldorf School,* Anthroposophic Press, New York 1995.

——, *Waldorf Education and Anthroposophy,* Volumes 1 and 2, Anthroposophic Press, New York 1995/6.

By Other Authors:

Anschütz, Marieke, *Children and Their Temperaments,* Floris Books, Edinburgh 1995.

Carlgren, Frans, *Education Towards Freedom: Rudolf Steiner Education: A Survey of the Work of Waldorf Schools throughout the World,* Lanthorn Press, East Grinstead 1993.

Childs, Gilbert, *Education and Beyond: Steiner and the Problems of Modern Society,* Floris Books, Edinburgh 1996.

—, *Steiner Education in Theory and Practice,* Floris Books, Edinburgh 1991.

Edmunds, L. Francis, *Renewing Education: Selected Writings on Steiner Education,* Hawthorn Press, Stroud 1992.

—, *Rudolf Steiner Education: The Waldorf School,* Rudolf Steiner Press, London 1992.

Finser, Torin, *School as a Journey: The Eight-Year Odyssey of a Waldorf Teacher and his Class,* Anthroposophic Press, New York 1994.

Gardner, John Fentress, *Education in Search of the Spirit: Essays on American Education,* Anthroposophic Press, New York 1996.

—, *Youth Longs to Know: Explorations of the Spirit in Education,* Anthroposophic Press, New York 1996.

Harwood, Cecil, *The Recovery of Man in Childhood,* The Myrin Institute of New York, New York 1992.

—, *The Way of a Child,* Rudolf Steiner Press, London 1997.

Heydebrand, Caroline von, *Childhood: A Study of the Growing Child,* Anthroposophic Press, New York 1995.

Jaffke, Freya, *Work and Play in Early Childhood,* Floris Books, Edinburgh 1996.

Lievegoed, Bernard, *Phases of Childhood: Growing in body, soul and spirit,* Floris Books, Edinburgh 1997.

Nobel, Agnes, *Educating through Art: The Steiner School Approach,* Floris Books, Edinburgh 1997.

Spock, Marjorie, *Teaching as a Lively Art,* Anthroposophic Press, New York 1985.

Useful addresses

United Kingdom
There are about 20 schools in the UK.
Further information from:
Steiner Schools Fellowship,
Kidbrooke Park
Forest Row
Sussex RH18 5JB
Fax 01342-826004

Ireland
There are 2 schools in Ireland.
Further information from
Steiner Schools Fellowship,
Kidbrooke Park
Forest Row
Sussex RH18 5JB U.K.
Fax 01342-826004

United States
There are about 100 schools in the United States.
Further information from:
Association of Waldorf Schools in North America
3911 Bannister Road
Fair Oaks CA 95628
Fax 916-961-0715

Canada
There are about 10 schools in Canada
Further information from:
Association of Waldorf Schools in North America
3911 Bannister Road
Fair Oaks CA 95628
Fax 916-961-0715

South Africa
There are about 8 schools in South Africa.
Further information from:
South African Federation of Waldorf Schools,
PO Box 67587
Bryanston 2021
Fax 011-792 1949

Australia
There are about 20 schools in Australia.
Further information from:
Association of Rudolf Steiner Schools in Australia
213 Wonga Road
Warranwood VIC 3134
Fax 03-9879-0820

New Zealand
There are 7 schools in New Zealand.
Further information from:
Federation of Rudolf Steiner Schools in New Zealand
PO Box 888
Hastings 4201
Fax 06-878-4160

There are also schools in
Western Europe (Austria, Belgium, France, Germany, Italy, Liechtenstein, Luxembourg, Netherlands, Portugal, Spain, Switzerland)
Northern Europe (Denmark,

Estonia, Finland, Latvia, Norway, Sweden)
Eastern Europe (Croatia, Czech Republic, Hungary, Poland, Romania. Russia, Slovenia)
Africa (Egypt, Kenya)
Latin America (Argentina, Brasil, Chile, Colombia, Ecuador, Mexico, Peru, Uruguay)
Asia (Israel, Japan)

Information from:
Bund der Freien Waldorfschulen
Heidehofstr 32
70184 Stuttgart
Germany
Fax +49-711-210 4219

Index